FROM ADDICTION
TO RECOVERY

FROM ADDICTION TO RECOVERY

✦

A THERAPIST'S PERSONAL JOURNEY

DR. ANITA GADHIA-SMITH
Foreword by Former Senator
Max Cleland

iUniverse, Inc.
New York Lincoln Shanghai

FROM ADDICTION TO RECOVERY
A THERAPIST'S PERSONAL JOURNEY

iUniverse books may be ordered through booksellers or by contacting:

iUniverse
2021 Pine Lake Road, Suite 100
Lincoln, NE 68512
www.iuniverse.com
1-800-Authors (1-800-288-4677)

Because of the dynamic nature of the Internet, any Web addresses or links contained in this book may have changed since publication and may no longer be valid.

ISBN: 978-0-595-46689-4 (pbk)
ISBN: 978-0-595-90984-1 (ebk)

Printed in the United States of America

TO MY GRANDFATHER, MANSUKHLAL JHAVERI

(1907–1981)

CONTENTS

ACKNOWLEDGMENTS

I AM GRATEFUL FOR CONTRIBUTIONS AND SUPPORT FROM THE FOLLOWING PEOPLE:

DR. RONALD E. SMITH
ANU GADHIA
LALIT H. GADHIA
KEVAL THAKKAR
JIGISHA THAKKAR
RAMESH H. GADHIA
DR. GEORGE KOLODNER
DR. SARAH H. PILLSBURY
BARBARA BLITZER
DONALD AUCOIN
CANDACE SAHM KOPIT
VINCENT VIRGA
INGE GUEN
CHRISTOPHER KENNEDY LAWFORD
KATHRYN SCOTT
JEANNINE WRAY
LEE MANLEY, JR.
TOM TUCKER
LORRAINE BOUSHELL
JACK HOVEY
SIDNEY GOLDREICH

FOREWORD

Very few therapists ever have the courage or feel the need to share the private side of their lives with others. Most are quite content with putting their best foot forward, putting a good face on things, especially mistakes and bad choices, and letting the world go on thinking what they want to think.

Not so for Dr. Anita Gadhia-Smith. She has to be brutally honest about her life or life kills her. That is the true reality of the human tragedy of addiction to drugs and alcohol, or in Anita's case, to them both. It's hell to disclose. It's hell to keep silent. Might as well let it all hang out.

And Anita does! But we are the beneficiaries of her brutal honesty. She shares the good, the bad, and the ugly about her journey through her personal background, drug and alcohol addiction, hitting bottom, seeking help, being single, getting married, and becoming a therapist in searching for a new life.

Anita is truly a wonderful healer—one who can heal because they have walked in the shoes of those they are trying to help. As such, she is able to give us insight to see that, as difficult and painful as our lives may be, there is light in the darkness. There is a way out of despair.

Very few have been where Anita has been and made it through the valley to the other side—alive. But because she made it—and is still making it—she gives us hope that we can make it too. Here's praying that we have the courage to walk in her footsteps.

Former U.S. Senator Max Cleland

INTRODUCTION

This book is written for anyone who is interested in alcoholism, addictions, the recovery process, relationships, or psychotherapy. My journey in sobriety is the greater part of the book, because I feel that my life really began after I got sober, even though I was twenty-seven years old at the time. Throughout the last seventeen years in recovery, I have experienced many phases of growth, along with numerous plateaus and unexpected changes.

The account of events is concise, yet full of important truths and growth experiences from my life. I have written this book with as much honesty as possible. It is a very personal description of how I got into active addiction, hit my bottom, and then grappled with a multitude of life issues both before and after getting sober. All of the events in this book are true, although I have changed some of the names of people and places, in order to preserve confidentiality.

Many more events have transpired in forty-five years than are recounted in this book. I have attempted to focus on those experiences that will be most helpful to the reader in understanding how to identify and break patterns of unhealthy behavior. I have focused on the progress that arose out of my difficulties and how everything ultimately contributed positively to my evolution. In addition to identifying negative behavior patterns, emphasis is directed towards the options and solutions that ultimately allowed ongoing progress, further growth, and positive development.

My formal education in psychology has been greatly enhanced by my life experience. Although I have had extensive clinical training as a psychotherapist, I believe that my personal experience has been equally powerful and irreplaceable in my education. In sharing my own life process, I hope that others will be able to benefit from my experience. As I discovered after getting into recovery, my issues extended beyond simply giving up drugs and alcohol. I hope that you will be able to identify with some aspects of my journey, and be inspired by others. Whatever you may be dealing with in your own life, there is nothing too great to overcome.

1

THE OUTSIDER

In India, Kshatriya is the royal and warrior caste. My ancient heritage was defined by this societal classification. Kshatriyas were kings, front-row fighters, and protectors of innocent people. The nature of my ancestral pedigree has been to battle and rule. In my life, I have always been a relentless warrior. In the face of adversity, persistence and a willingness to stick with doing whatever is necessary have been the fundamental nature of my existence. I inherited these qualities from my lineage.

My parents moved to the United States from India in 1961 to attend graduate school at the University of Maryland. My mother, Anu Jhaveri, comes from a prominent literary family. My maternal grandfather, Mansukhlal Jhaveri, was a renowned literary figure and an educator in India. He was a professor of Gujarati at St. Xavier's College in Bombay, and also served as a college principal in Porbundar, India. His literary accomplishments included eight volumes of poetry in the Gujarati language, several literary criticism books, five volumes on Gujarati grammar and its history, and several translations of Sanskrit and Shakespearean classics into the Gujarati language. He was recognized in the World Book of Who's Who as an accomplished author.

My father, Lalit Gadhia, is the eldest son of seven children from a large, orthodox Hindu, Gujarati family from Bombay that had made its fortune in the chemical business. He met my mother because he had read my grandfather's books and consequently attended St. Xavier's College in Bombay in order to study under him. He approached my mother one day when he was running for an elected office at the college and asked for her vote. She more than voted for him. They got engaged in Bombay and then moved to the United States in 1961 to get married and begin a new life together. Their marriage was the only one in history from either side of the family that was not an arranged marriage.

I am an only child. I was born in Washington, D.C. on June 13, 1962, and was raised in Baltimore, Maryland. I attended Friends School, a private Quaker institution. I began at Friends in nursery school when I was four years old, and went there all the way through the end of high school, fourteen years in all. Friends was one of the very best schools in the city. Most of the students were from middle to upper class professional families who lived near the school in the surrounding posh neighborhoods of Guilford, Roland Park, and Homeland.

When I started at Friends, both of my parents were working at Community Action Agency, a federally-funded anti-poverty program. My mother had done graduate studies in sociology, and my father was an economist. As they both worked full-time, I would go to and from school by bus, and then to my babysitter's house after school until my mother got home from work. My father generally left very early in the morning, and was usually not home until well after dinner. It was rare that the three of us ever spent an evening together as a family.

By the time I was six, things were really not going well at home. My parents were experiencing enormous conflict and difficulty. My father was having an affair with his secretary, Susan. My parents and Susan all worked together at Community Action Agency and Susan also knew my mother quite well. Things got very, very messy. The combination of my father's two extracurricular activities, politics and Susan, kept him out of the house virtually all the time. As my mother did not drive a car, we were totally dependent upon my father for mobility. His absence significantly limited our activities and contributed to a shared sense of dependency and helplessness.

My mother was distraught and terrified that the marriage was ending. She had been raised in traditional Indian society where these things were inconceivable. In India, you got married, and stayed married for life—no matter what. There was simply no other option. At home in

India, the families would not have allowed a divorce to occur. Societal and family pressures were simply too powerful to escape. You never really separated psychologically from your family of origin. My father's family lived as a joint family, with his parents, all the brothers, sisters, their spouses and children under one roof.

Here in the United States, however, it was possible to break free of the family. When my father was finally liberated from his family's watchful eye, he chose to live an untamed life. My mother was shocked and dismayed because this was not the man she had known and married back in India. She had no help or reference points to guide her through this journey. Despite family pressure from distant India to stay together, my parents could not work things out, and when I was six years old, they separated. My father packed his bags for a business trip to California, and never came back. Eventually, they divorced.

My father's family in India could not easily accept the divorce. They were extremely traditional, and were very prominent in Bombay society. No one in the entire history of the family had ever divorced, and this brought shame upon the Gadhia name. My paternal grandfather was a revered patriarch and leader in the community. He went to my mother's father, the very renowned author and literary figure, and begged for forgiveness for what his son had done to his daughter. He literally bent down and kissed his feet. Eventually, everyone realized that there was no saving the marriage. It was going to end no matter what anyone said or did.

How did I feel through this time? Alone. There was no one there for me. My father was gone, and my mother was having a nervous breakdown. I would see my mother crying her eyes out, and beating her own legs black and blue with her fists. She was in a state of utter devastation and major depression, which would require a long term healing process. There were a series of several women who came to live with us for long periods of time, because my mother was not emotionally stable. They were friends of the family who were willing to come and stay with us out of concern and goodwill. My mother's pain was so overwhelming that mine was imperceptible to anyone, most of all to me.

As an only child, I have always struggled with my loneliness and simultaneous need for space. One the one hand, I have always been a very lonely person. This drove me to seek out the company of many companions. On the other hand, I have always had a need for solitude and breathing room of my own. This has been a recurrent internal conflict over my lifetime. Very early on, I intuitively sensed my aloneness in the universe. Many people come to realize this in midlife, but I first noticed it when I was about six.

I learned very early on to deny my feelings. I told myself for many years that I was not at all affected by the divorce, and that I was just fine. I became focused on taking care of my mother's feelings, and becoming her confidant. She leaned on me. I needed her, but she was not fully emotionally available to me due to her own distress. I also longed for my father, and desperately wanted him in my life. I was very sad, because I had always been very close to my father, and was now cut off from him. I truly felt in the middle. My parents were embroiled in bitter conflict. I loved both of them so much, yet felt divided in my heart.

In one significant area, my parents were in agreement. They both believed strongly in providing me with a solid educational foundation at Friends School. In India, education was the route to upward mobility. They wanted me to have a firm base from which to build a successful life. It turns out that they were absolutely right.

The years at Friends School were the fundamental building blocks of who I would ultimately become. I grew up with solid people who had ethics, family values, intelligence and integrity. I did not fully appreciate the experience while I was there, but now I can see how essential it was. After their divorce, there were financial struggles, but my mother continued to contribute a large portion of her salary so that I could continue my private school education without interruption.

Yet, the entire time I was at Friends School, I felt like an outsider looking in. I always felt that somehow I did not quite belong. I felt painfully different. I was caught between two cultures. I am of East Indian descent; everyone else there was American. My mother wore a sari at that time, the traditional dress in India. It is a beautiful and feminine garment that looked exquisite on her, but I felt that our ethnicity set me apart from everyone else. Like many other Indian women of her generation, she did not drive. This limitation also set me apart from the others. I desperately wanted to belong, and to be accepted. I wanted my mother to dress like the other mothers. I wanted her to drive a car, so that we could be independent like the other families. I wanted to be like everyone else.

I used to try to dress in the style of my preppie classmates, but it was not quite me. I secretly wished that I was tall and blond and idolized anyone who was. I was not really one of them. I could try to look and act the part, but I felt like I was pretending to be something I was not. When I went to India, the people there called me an American. When I was in the United States, people called me Indian. The question was: What was I? I had no idea.

I felt defective. I did not want to be different from my friends in school. This presented an insurmountable challenge, because I was different in almost every way. I was dark-haired and olive-skinned instead of wasp-looking. My parents were divorced instead of married. I lived in an apartment instead of a house. We had limited financial resources, while many of my friends were wealthy. I had idealized the "regular" American families that I saw all around me. I always felt that if people really knew me, they would know that I really did not measure up to their standards of "normal," and would reject me.

I remember going to visit my friends at their homes and wishing I had their lives. I would fantasize about being this person or that person. I constantly compared myself to others, and came up short in my mind. They all seemed to be living abundant lives, while mine felt deprived, barren and miserable. Their lives appeared to be so much superior to mine, so much more normal. I was excruciatingly lonely and deeply ashamed of my parents' difficulties. I felt flawed and unconsciously blamed myself for the family problems.

Bringing together my two cultures in my internal world was a major issue. I did not realize that I even could bring them together. This created a split that would later become a theme for many other areas of my life. As a young person, I thought that I had to choose between the two cultures and two parents. I did not know that I could love both cultures, both parents and take the best from all of them in my life. Given the fact that I was in the United States, it seemed that the best cultural option was to try to be as American as possible and find a sense of belonging in this culture.

This caused me to reject my Indian heritage completely. I did not want even a trace of it in my life. I felt that this would only take away from what I was trying to be. Thus, I was repelled by anything that was at all Indian. I avoided Indian food, clothing, and goods. I looked down on my own heritage with condescension. This led to a sense of self-hatred, which fueled my negative feelings and behaviors for many years to come. I did everything I possibly could to escape myself, my family, and the confusion of my internal world.

I did not feel a sense of belonging in my own family because it had never been cohesive. It had come apart. Unfortunately, I was so far away from most of my relatives in India that, even though I would have felt a greater sense of belonging if I had been with them, I did not see them often enough to internalize any sense of family unity. I went to visit India once every few years and felt enormous love from both sides of my family every time, but it was very brief. I would then return back home to my aloneness and separateness.

I was sad and depressed about what had happened in the family, and had no way to process my feelings. As time went on, my mother and I started to have conflict and difficulty in our relationship. I unconsciously and unjustly blamed her for the divorce, even though it was not her fault. I saw her as the "loser" and did everything I could to be unlike her and to emulate my father. I missed my father terribly. I had been very attached to him as a child, and I was grieving the loss of him in my daily life. I internalized all the chaos and hurt, and carried a huge burden of pain inside. The pain went deeper and deeper inside until I could not recognize or access it consciously. It just became an encrusted part of me. I denied the pain to myself and to everyone else. I kept on saying: "I'm fine."

I looked like my father physically, and reflected his behaviors and attitudes. This was a constant reminder to my mother of the man she resented for devastating her life. Not only was I in conflict with my mother, but I was also in the middle of the discord between my parents, and there was nothing I could do to improve the situation. I remember secretly wishing I could fix their problems and get them back together. It is probably this wish that to some extent fueled my later desire to become a therapist and to develop expertise in working with couples.

My father was unable to spend much time with me because of their struggles. I felt like a weapon used by my parents to hurt one another. This added to my own anger and feelings of alienation. Although my parents were not able to have a harmonious relationship, they were civil when we were together. My father would come to visit me at my mother's house once a week and have a meal with us in the kitchen in order to spend some time together. Unfortunately, it was not enough. But it was better than nothing.

The divided loyalties that result from divorce generate a fragmented sense of self. When I was with my father, I was on his side. When I was with my mother, I was on her side. I understood both of their feelings and points of view. Both perspectives were valid. How could this be? How does an eight-year-old integrate all this chaos without any help? It was very confusing.

I did not feel like I really knew who I was or what I thought. What I thought and felt was determined by whomever I was with at the time. I was a chameleon who always wanted to please the person in front of me in order to seek their approval. I never got in touch with my own opinions and feelings. This became an increasingly uncomfortable existence. I started to develop anxiety-related compulsive behaviors, which were manifested on a daily basis. I carried around all the internal chaos until I found relief.

2

LOOKING AT LIFE
THROUGH A STRAW

I was introduced to alcohol at a very young age. My father was very European in his habits, and consumed wine as part of the daily dining experience. At age three, I was given small sips of sherry at my parents' dinner parties. I first remember being intoxicated at age eight when I went out to Vellegia's Restaurant for an Italian lunch with my parents. This was the awakening of the alcoholic shadow.

I felt a fire-like feeling in my throat. When the white wine reached my stomach, I got a feeling of lightness in my head that felt like I had finally come home. Moments after the wine had penetrated my system, I realized that this feeling was what I had been looking for and missing my whole life. It was relief. All of a sudden, I did not feel crazy anymore. I felt normal. When I discovered alcohol, I was able to escape from the chaos inside myself for the first time ever.

The first time that I put my mind to getting drunk, I was eleven years old. I really did a bang up job of it. My mother went out to the store, and I raided her liquor cabinet. I started guzzling massive quantities of straight hard liquor from tall tumblers. I gulped down several different varieties of whiskey, rum, gin, and scotch, straight out of the bottles. The liquor tasted awful, but I did not care. I wanted to escape. I drank so much so quickly that I blacked out within minutes, and have no recollection of what then transpired. What I do remember, however, is waking up in the hospital. I came to at Union Memorial Hospital, and had no idea what had happened or how I got there.

I asked the nurse, "What am I doing here?"

She said, "You drank too much and hurt your head."

"What do you mean?" I asked.

"You hit your head on something at home, and you have twelve stitches in your forehead," she said.

"Are my parents mad at me?" I quivered.

"Don't worry. They are not angry with you. You're going to be okay. You're a lucky girl. This could have been much worse," she said.

"Did I ruin the shirt that I was wearing?" I asked.

"There is a lot of blood on it; I don't think it will come out."

What was really disturbing about this incident was that the thing I was most upset about was ruining my shirt. I had just gotten a new shirt from the Merry-Go-Round boutique, and I was very proud of it. It made me feel "cool." It was a light blue polyester shirt, with pictures of fish on it and straps that tied in the back. I was devastated that I had only been able to wear the shirt once and now it was ruined.

I was not the least bit concerned about my head injury or the alcohol poisoning that I had just survived. I was not even alarmed that this incident had happened. In fact, I could not wait to drink again. I wanted more anesthetic. I was relieved to discover that there was an escape from the hell I had been living inside myself.

In the coming months, I eagerly anticipated weekly meals out with my father because I was allowed to have a couple of beers with him over lunch. We used to go out every Saturday afternoon for dosas at the India House Restaurant. There was always laughter and lively intellectual discussion with one or two of his buddies. It was the high point of my life. I got to see my father, and I also got to drink. It was a double winner. This bonded me with my father around alcohol and getting high, and also fed my blossoming relationship with alcohol.

It did not take that much to get intoxicated. A couple of beers would do the trick. I also started buying my own beer at the age of thirteen. I looked older and more mature than my age, and I was able to buy beer and wine in several of the local package goods stores. I was very proud of the fact that I was able to get my own alcohol. My self-reliance was working to get me what I wanted, access to alcohol.

As time passed, I continued to seek out people and situations that involved drinking and drugs. Melanie was my best friend in elementary and middle school. She was tall, blond, and charismatic. She attracted a lot of older boys, who found her irresistible. She was very mature for her age and knew how to use what she had. She had friends who were much older, and who had taught her about adult activities. She introduced me to smoking marijuana, the Rolling Stones, and older boys. These soon turned out to be my favorite things in life.

By the time I was thirteen, I had discovered life on the wild side. Once I got a taste of it, there was no turning back. This was the life I had been looking for all along, but did not know it. It was the era of sex, drugs, and rock-and-roll. Freedom and experimentation were a way of life. Using drugs and alcohol as the gateway to new experiences now became my main objective. I had meaning and purpose.

Melanie and I were inseparable for several years. I finally had a best friend that completed me. My lack of selfhood was made whole by internalizing her identity. She was from a wealthy family and lived in a beautiful home. Although her parents were divorced like mine were, her former-model, Hungarian mother was remarried to a successful businessman. She seemed to have it all; beauty, success, and the finer things in life. I idolized everything about her and wanted to emulate her in every possible way. We looked good together when we went out to meet guys. Between the two of us, we attracted a lot of attention and adventures.

When I was not in school, I would drink with kids in the neighborhood who were from "the other side of the fence"- literally. I lived on the edge of a posh neighborhood called Homeland which bordered a more working-class neighborhood called Govans. On the other side of the fence of the apartment complex where my mother and I lived were scores of "rough" kids who were only too happy to drink and smoke pot with me. I remember seeing them through the fence, and wanting to escape my wall of isolation. I had to climb over the fence to get to hang out with them. We would go to nearby wooded areas to drink and smoke pot. The woods were our safe, private haven.

This was the first of many groups of lower companions whom I would seek out in order to feel better about myself. I did not feel that I could measure up to my private school friends because of my low self-esteem. I thought that my "straight" friends were boring and childish, while the street crowd was more interesting and exciting. If I could feel superior to the people I hung out with, then I could be on top, and I did not have to face my feelings of being "less than," which were so prevalent with my school friends.

After middle school, Melanie had gotten herself into a lot of trouble with the school. A major difference between Melanie and I was that my grades were excellent—mostly A's, even though I was high on marijuana most of the time. She did not have very good grades, and that was a deal-breaker at Friends. They had very high academic standards. Her performance was poor, and the school knew that she was using drugs and being a bad influence on the other kids. She was not invited to return back to Friends for high school, and I was not permitted to have further contact with her. I was devastated by the loss of another key person in my life. From this point forward, I was on my own. No more Melanie. However, I was so well established in my wild ways and drug-using that I had no problem continuing to go down the wrong path without her.

I found secret places at school and in the surrounding woods where I could go to smoke pot without getting caught. I was amazed that I had not gotten caught by the school, and that I was permitted to remain at Friends. I attribute this to my sneakiness and deceptive abilities. My good grades also kept me from having to face myself and what I was doing. There are three obstacles to overcoming addiction: great intelligence, great beauty, and great wealth. I had the first two, which were enough to keep me going down the road of addiction for a very long time. This was the beginning of my belief that if I kept everything looking okay on the outside, then I was okay.

By the time I was in high school, I was smoking pot around the clock. When I woke up, getting high was the first thing I did in the morning. I would stick my head out of my bedroom window every morning and take a few hits to get going. Then I smoked several times throughout the day to keep the high constant. Before going to sleep at night, I would smoke again. I would even wake up in the middle of the night and smoke myself back to sleep.

My goal was to never be straight, unless it was absolutely necessary. On some days, I bought alcohol and drank in the alleys while I was walking to school. Sometimes, I would show up drunk at school at 8:00 in the morning and barely be able to walk down the flights of stairs in between floors. I had a relentless will to stay high or drunk all the time. Because of my ability to perform well in school, I got away with it.

My best friend in high school was a gay Iranian boy named Moshe. He and I had a couple of big things in common. We were both of foreign ancestry (he was a descendent of the Shah of Iran), and we were both outsiders. Moshe felt twice as much the outsider because of being gay. We spent a lot of time together, hanging out, smoking pot, and reading fashion magazines. He bought me my first mammoth September issue of Vogue, and I was hooked on magazines after that. Moshe worked in a downtown restaurant as a waiter, and was "out" in the world as a gay boy. Because of Moshe, I discovered that gay men made really good "girlfriends." In some ways they were even better than actual girlfriends. There was no jealousy or competition. He adored women. We wanted completely different things, yet we still wanted many of the same things. We had a lot in common.

Around this time, I moved in with my father. I did not plan or announce my move. I just gradually started spending more and more nights on his couch. I was desperate to get out of my mother's house. She and I were in such conflict that we could barely speak. I was in full-force rebellion, and there was no way that I was going to give up. I wanted to do what I wanted to do. I was not going to let anyone control me. I wanted to discover the world beyond Friends School, and nothing could stop me.

Just before the end of high school, I went out one night to Tiffany's, the hottest disco in town. Tiffany's was the definition of glamorous. It was Baltimore's equivalent of Studio 54. All the beautiful people went there. It was 1979. Disco was hot, hot, hot. Sex was free and easy. Drugs were everywhere. Music was the pulse of life. Tiffany's had it all under one roof. I was amazed when I saw an old friend at Tiffany's. It was Melanie, my old childhood friend from Friends School who had gotten kicked out many years earlier. I had not been able to get in touch with her since she had left Friends.

Here she was all grown up—and a mess. She was not quite as awesome as I had remembered her as a child. She had gained weight, looked somewhat unkempt, and did not seem very intelligent or articulate. She told wild and unbelievable stories about having sex with movie actors and rock stars to try to impress us. I was not sure if I even believed her. I intuitively felt that she may have been making it all up, which just seemed pathetic. I saw her in a new light. For the first time, she just seemed like a sad person, a pretender, and a fake. She was no longer the glamorous femme fatale that I had wanted to emulate. Something had gone terribly wrong with Melanie. She did not seem to be blossoming very well.

That night, Melanie introduced me to her beautiful brown-eyed, light blond-haired friend named Scott. Scott was four years my senior. He was a very energetic, confident, take-charge guy. Although he was not a big guy, he was brazen and mighty. She was out with Scott that night, but he was not her boyfriend. They invited me to go back to Scott's house to party and do cocaine. I could not believe that after all these years; I had reconnected with Melanie. I had wondered about her for so long. I never thought I would see her again. Melanie said that she lived in Los Angeles, and was about to leave town to go home. That was the last time I ever saw her. I still wonder about her to this day.

Scott invited me to go out with him to celebrate my upcoming eighteenth birthday. I accepted his offer, and did not know how much this invitation would ultimately alter the course of my life. He had a strong appetite for hard drugs and lots of them, despite physiological limitations imposed upon him by childhood diabetes. He was constantly monitoring his blood sugar and trying to maintain his equilibrium. Keeping himself in balance was practically impossible when he drank, but more doable with drugs—or so he thought.

He loved to play, and had lots of time and money to do so. I was never quite clear as to how he made his money, but he always had more. He was a wheeler dealer, and then some. He owned a VW rabbit and a motorcycle. He lived in the luxurious basement suite of his parents' custom-built home in a wooded suburb of Baltimore near Lake Roland. His family was fairly wealthy, and had set him up nicely. He even had a sauna in his bathroom, something I had never seen before.

For our first date, Scott had a special celebration planned. We did high-test cocaine for several hours to warm up for the night and then attempted to go out to dinner to a nice Italian restaurant in Little Italy. What a joke. Eating food does not mix well with cocaine. It was virtually impossible to get even one bite of food down in our cocaine frenzy, but we went through the motions and tried anyway.

Neither one of us could enjoy eating dinner, so we left to go out for a couple of drinks at a downtown jazz club to try to take the edge off the cocaine. We had gotten a little too wired. The night of my eighteenth birthday was the first time I had done this much cocaine, and it was a very potent experience. My mind and body were racing so fast that hours went by in the blink of an eye. I could not stop talking. I could not stop wanting more—just one more line and then just one more and then one more. There was no end to the craving for another bump.

The thing about cocaine is that when you go up, you only feel really good for about the first ten minutes. At first you feel self-assured, assertive, and invincible. Then the superhuman feeling of elevation quickly changes to a nervous feeling of anxiety, depletion and then deep depression accompanied by psychotic paranoia. The only way out of the cocaine depression is to do more cocaine. The more you do, the crazier it gets. The craving to do more is fueled by the desire to avoid the cocaine depression crash, which intensifies with more use. Eventually you end up so wired that you do not even know what happened to you, how much money you spent, or what day it is anymore. Hours go by like minutes. This goes on and on and on, until you run out. That is when it gets really challenging.

The paranoia that occurs during the cocaine crash is mind-blowing. You think you hear people coming to your door. You think that people are outside looking into your house. You are sure that someone is coming to get you. Your mind obsesses over the paranoia for hours on end, and there is no way to stop it. There is no way to control your mind, which has now become your worst enemy. The only thing you can do is wait it out in misery, or take another drug to bring you down. Alcohol was the easiest way to accomplish this. After a few drinks, I would calm down, then crave more cocaine and get too high again, then crave something to bring me down again, and then want to go back up again. The cycle was endless.

Although I was technically living with my father, I started staying at Scott's house most nights, and we were pretty much inseparable, except when I had commitments at college. I was drawn into his world of drugs, shady characters, and nonstop excitement. There were always people around his house that I had never seen before who were either buying or selling drugs. I never knew what treat was going to be available that day, or what new experience I would have.

One day, Scott had a bag of 1,000 Percodan pain killers. I took two of them, and found a new love—opiates. I got a warm feeling in my body and soul, and had the refreshing sense that everything in the world was perfect. This was a feeling I had never known before. It was better than all the other drugs I had tried put together. The euphoric sense of well-being was incredible. It was what I had always been looking for. I liked that fact that the pills were small, easy to hide, and more predictable and controllable than street drugs. I also liked the fact that they calmed my natural anxiety. Up to this point, I had been drinking and smoking pot daily, and had used LSD and cocaine on occasion. Opiates were a new breed of drugs that stood unsurpassed.

As Scott and I became a couple, I crossed a threshold and entered into a much bigger world. For the first time, I began to see and experience life as never before. Up to this point, my existence had been fairly sheltered in the Friends school and Homeland neighborhood cocoon. I had begun to explore Baltimore nightlife, but was still a novice in most areas of life. Scott had been out in life a great deal. He had experience with underground worlds that I never even knew existed. I could handle anything if he was leading the way.

3

FUN AND GAMES

One of Scott's friends told us about a new commercial real estate development project opening on July 2, 1980 at Baltimore's Inner Harbor. It was called Harborplace. This project consisted of two large pavilions on the water, housing shops and restaurants. Baltimore had never seen a tourist attraction like this before. This was the up-and-coming hot spot in town, and we all decided to go there and apply for jobs. I had just graduated from high school, and I was eager to experience more of life.

I was hired at an Indian restaurant called Tandoor by a young Indian woman named Mona. She was beautiful and gracious. Within a few minutes of our initial meeting, we started trading shampoo secrets, shoe preferences, and other girl talk. At that time, I was eighteen and she was twenty-one. Although she was my boss, Mona also became a very good friend. We looked somewhat alike, and people always thought we were the same person. She and I had an instant connection that would ultimately last a lifetime.

It is curious that I chose to work at an Indian restaurant, when I could have worked in at least twenty other establishments in the area. My belief is that I was unconsciously trying to connect with my heritage. I gravitated towards the Indian restaurant because there was a big part of my identity that needed healing. This was required in order to let go of some of my self-loathing and lack of self-acceptance. Although I had spent my entire life trying to prove to myself that I was American, I also really needed to become part of something Indian. Working at Tandoor was the perfect resolution to this conflict.

A short while later Mona hired Veena as the restaurant hostess. Although Veena and Mona were both a few years older than me, the three of us bonded and became the sisters that none of us had ever had. I had no siblings and had spent my entire life until this point having few ties to my family's Indian culture and roots. Mona and Veena both had brothers, but no sisters. The friendships with

Mona and Veena were the universe's way of giving me sisters. This was also the beginning of having a connection with my own cultural heritage.

Being a waitress was exactly what I needed to come out of my shell. I had been painfully self-conscious and shy as a child. Waitressing gave me practice at interacting and speaking with large numbers of diverse people. This resulted in the development of greatly-needed social skills. I became much more of an extrovert, and got more comfortable relating to people during this time.

The other thing that was great about the restaurant business was the drinking. The restaurant scene tends to attract people who like to drink. The staff usually went out drinking somewhere after working the dinner shift, so there were built-in drinking companions. At Harborplace, there were many fun places to go without traveling very far. Sometimes we even got to drink after work at our restaurant. This life felt like paradise. The normal routine was to work, make some cash, go out drinking after work, then end up slightly further uptown at Tiffany's disco, and even possibly at an after-hours party at someone's house.

All of this was concurrent with dating Scott and starting college at The Johns Hopkins University. Despite my active addiction and daily drug use in high school, I was admitted to one of the nation's most prestigious universities. I had managed to keep my addiction lurking under the surface, so that no one around me realized that I was ill. Because I had performed so well in school, my addiction was invisible. Addicts can be deep into their addiction, and still be very high-functioning.

At Hopkins orientation, one of the first people I met was Alex. He was a tall, blond, very intelligent older transfer student who was living with his European girlfriend. I was immediately drawn to Alex, and we became fast friends. It was not too long before I learned that Alex was an older student because his studies had been delayed by having been in rehab for drug addiction for an extended period of time. How did we addicts keep finding each other? Out of a crowd of hundreds of people, Alex and I found each other the way that two tigers would find one another in a crowd of elephants. Addicts and alcoholics tend to gravitate towards one another, whether they are using or not.

As I went through my first year of college, I went to classes during the day, when I was not too hung-over to show up. I was working nights at Tandoor, going out afterwards, and spending the rest of my time using with Scott and getting high. I was still living with my father, but I was hardly ever there. I loved that he did not try to control me, and basically let me do whatever I wanted to do. That suited me just fine. I was enjoying my new life of freedom and independence.

In 1980, Hopkins was predominantly male, and had only been admitting female students for a limited number of years. Thus, there were many more males than females. Most of the student body was comprised of premed boys from New York and New Jersey. I loved the gender ratio, because it increased my romantic possibilities. I was flamboyant, and part of a small group of attractive girls, so I became well-known fairly quickly. Most of the girls there were fairly studious and nerdy, so there was not much competition. In the entire undergraduate student body, you could count the attractive people of both sexes on two hands.

In the spring semester of freshman year at Hopkins, I wore black fishnet stockings and a skirt one day to class. I saw a beautiful boy among the crowd of other students, and we made eye contact. He was definitely checking me out. I had never seen anyone this handsome in my life. I had to know him. He said that he introduced himself to me because he loved my stockings, and thought it was outrageous that I chose to wear them to my early morning economics class. His name was Mark.

Mark was the most handsome boy I had ever seen in my life. He had dirty blond hair, green eyes, and a beautiful build. His jaw line was prominent and gave his face a striking angular shape. He looked like a Calvin Klein model. Mark was from New Jersey, and was the son of a prominent architect. He was fairly sheltered, and had not done many drugs. I introduced him to codeine cough syrup and Percodan, which he loved. The warm, cozy sensation from opiates was even more delicious with a sweetie like Mark.

We started to spend time together, and I became his college girlfriend. But wait, I already had a boyfriend, didn't I? I did not let that stop me. For the next two years, I had two simultaneous relationships. I managed to keep them apart, and basically led two lives—my college life with Mark (the golden boy), and my underground hard-core drug-centered life with Scott (the bad boy). My entire existence was wrapped around the two guys in my life, and using substances. Both were centered on the same things, self-indulgence and feeling good.

I needed my waitressing job to fund my addiction and satisfy my need for attention from people. I had never been one of the "popular" girls at Friends. I had always been an outsider. Although I was pretty, I had never gotten attention from the boys I had known at Friends. We were the same age, but I was light years ahead in development. At this point, my self-esteem was low and my sense of self-worth depended on approval and attention from others.

I was now meeting multitudes of new people and getting an unimaginable amount of attention from men from all walks of life. Some were guys who came into the restaurant, others were passers-by, and still others were from the downtown nightlife crowd. I was photographed regularly for tourism magazines and by many visitors to Harborplace who walked past the restaurant. Mona, Veena, and I were a trio of sari-clad tourist attractions who were stunningly beautiful. We had a happening scene at Tandoor. I had arrived.

4

GOING DOWN

I continued to sink more deeply into my addiction throughout college. I crossed lines that I had never planned on crossing. One day, I was at Scott's house and he went out to get some cocaine. When he returned, we ceremoniously cut up our white lines of powder. I did my line, but this time, something was different. I did not go up; I felt relaxed and euphoric instead. I started to get the warmest, happiest feeling I had ever had in my life. All of a sudden, I loved everything, and was comfortable with the world; all was well. It dawned on me that this was not like any cocaine that I had ever had.

I said to Scott, "What is going on here? This doesn't feel like coke."

"It's not coke," he said.

"What do you mean? What is this?"

"It's heroin," Scott said.

"Why didn't you tell me what it was before I did it? I didn't want to do heroin. I wanted coke," I said.

"Because I knew that if I told you what it was, you wouldn't do it."

I felt betrayed and was stunned that this had happened. At the same time, I was pleased, because I loved the high. This was better than any other drug. Nothing compared to this new feeling of bliss and well-being. It was shocking, because I had thought of heroin as the worst thing a person could possibly do. Heroin-users were low-life scum and degenerates, not well-bred, intelligent lovely people like me.

Because of crossing my own line, I immediately felt a sense of shame that was on a deeper level. It stemmed from a sense self-betrayal. Using heroin was something I had told myself I would never do, under any circumstances. Now that I had done it and liked it, I was not so sure that it was such a bad idea.

At this point, I did not seek it out again. But I never forgot how good it was. Pot, alcohol, pills, cough syrup, mushrooms, LSD, and cocaine were a daily order of business until the end of college. It was always possible to get something on a regular basis. I felt okay with myself because I maintained good enough grades to keep making it through my undergraduate classes at Johns Hopkins. Hopkins was not an easy school, so I thought that I was doing alright.

It was much easier to take classes that started late in the day, because it was so difficult to get up early after a late night of partying. Even then, I usually did not attend classes unless there was an exam that required me to be there. I generally only showed up for my school obligations when it was critical. Work was a different story; I was always there and always on time. I felt that as long as I kept my commitments and fulfilled my obligations, I was a responsible person who was managing life well. I was working full-time and also taking a full load in school. Because I was still functioning at such a high level, I remained in denial about the progression of my disease. This kept me from having to face my addiction, which was continually getting worse.

Around this time, I had a parting of the ways with both Scott and Mark. I became bored with Scott and wanted to expand my prospects in order to experience different people. We drifted apart, but stayed friends and were in contact occasionally. After spending his junior year abroad in Paris, something happened to Mark. He became "bisexual," which, to me was code for becoming gay. When he returned to Hopkins in his senior year, he started spending time at the Oasis, Baltimore's premiere gay disco. His primary companion was Dennis, a wealthy, fat, gay hairdresser who was using coke as bait to catch him. This was not my scene. I could not deal with it. Mark and I grew distant.

I eventually got fired from Tandoor after a three-day drinking binge with my friend Claudio, which culminated in my showing up for work drunk and dropping a full tray of food for four people on the floor. I was entirely too drunk to go to work, but in my compulsive commitment to be responsible, I showed up and blew it in a big way. Staff and customers complained about me, and my dear friend Mona had no choice but to let me go. I understood why.

Within two days of being fired from Tandoor, I secured another waitressing job at a nearby downtown pub, Billy's, which was a drinking scene extraordinaire. Claudio was friendly with owners, and got me the job since I had lost my job at Tandoor as the result of our drinking binge. Billy's was the preppy drinking haven on Thursday nights in downtown Baltimore. Although the money was not as good, this job was even better in some ways because both co-owners loved to drink.

Drinking was not only accepted, but even encouraged in the work environment. In fact, one night a week, all the restaurant chairs and tables were removed, so that the entire place could be transformed into one giant drink-fest bar scene. These were my kind of people. I could finally drink with more ease and comfort at work. I made more drinking and partying friends as a result of this new job. I was also still actively involved in the downtown bar and after-hours club scene when I got off of work.

My favorite place to go after getting off from Billy's was Horizon. It was very unique as far as bars go. The fifties red décor was seedy and humble, but it was not uncommon to see Hollywood movie stars and other famous people stop by for a drink. It had an artsy, eclectic flavor, which was always interesting an unpredictable. This was the sort of place where strippers had danced on the bar in the 40's and 50's. A new co-owner had come on board and transformed the clientele to a younger, more diverse group of people. It was definitely the in-crowd place.

It was the only bar I had ever seen that housed every type of person from all walks of life under one roof. There were wealthy, poor, educated, working-class, gay, straight, bisexual, students, artists, and businessmen. You never knew who would be there. That made it really exciting. Usually the after-bar crowd from all over the city would also end up there on the way home. This made last call at the end of the night the best part of any day.

Towards the end of college, I landed a job at Horizon as a bartender. I had kept up a good GPA at Hopkins, where I had studied French Literature and Humanities. Since I had no clear plan about where to go next, there was no more glamorous job that I could imagine than working at the most popular club in Baltimore. I did not know how to bartend, but I did not let that stop me. I had waitressed, and figured that I could learn as I went, which is exactly what happened. It was not too difficult.

As a waitress, it was often necessary to go behind the bar to make drinks. Bartending was merely an expansion of what I had already done. When I did not know something, I could just ask my co-bartender for help. He was a slick, well-seasoned bartender who was also in the juke-box rental and cigarette vending machine business. He knew all the ropes of the bar and restaurant business and was only too happy to serve as a mentor. He loved the scene at the bar and made working behind the bar a nightly show-time event. We were the main stars of the show, and the bar crowd was the adoring audience.

The customers were very regular and loyal. Most of them came into the bar four or five nights a week. Many of them were alcoholics whose lives revolved around the social scene of the bar. The club was their life. They revered the bartenders like doctors. We had what they wanted, and they tried to please us and stay in our good graces in order to get served. There was a lot of competition to actually get a drink, because on most nights, the bar crowd was four rows of people deep. It was a very busy, thriving place that attracted people from all over the country. I once went to New York City, and someone on the street asked me if I was the bartender from Horizon in Baltimore. This happened everywhere I went, in the most unlikely places, and it never ceased to amaze me. It was like being a celebrity.

My best girlfriend and confidante was Madeline, a petite version of Kim Basinger. I had originally met Madeline when I had worked at Tandoor and she had worked at the Powder Room, a makeup store at Harborplace. We were yin and yang; light and dark-haired opposites, who attracted a lot of attention. Madeline and I went out drinking together on a regular basis. We had many after-hours adventures and were each others' lifelines through my adult years in Baltimore. Over the years, we had kept in touch and developed a long-lasting friendship. We spoke nearly every day for years.

There were guys who would come to Horizon just to hang out and watch people, including the bartenders. There was one guy named Brendan who came in almost every day and just drank coffee and soda. He was a strikingly handsome Irish man, very tall and muscular. He reminded me of Clark Kent in the old Superman movies.

I could feel his penetrating gaze from across the bar. His expression was serious. I always had the feeling that something big would happen if I ever got to know him. He had a very powerful vibe. He was always alone, and never drank alcohol. After a while, I could feel from his relentless stare that he had feelings for me. One night, I was drinking heavily after work, and I invited him to come home with me. He accepted my invitation.

In the blink of an eye, I was in a new relationship. We were together every single day. We drank together, although Brendan had confessed that he had been sober for quite a few months before he met me. Thanks to meeting me, he was now drinking again. One night fairly early on, we got really, really drunk and ended up having a big ugly fight. Brendan told me that I had a serious problem with alcohol, and that I needed to do something about it. He insisted that we both stop drinking, or he was going to break up with me. I had to choose between Brendan and alcohol. I reluctantly chose Brendan.

5

LIVING ON THE EDGE

The next day, Brendan took me to my first recovery meeting. I walked out after a few minutes because I did not feel that I belonged with the down-and-out crowd of old, emphysema-ridden, crotchety men that I saw there. I was twenty-three, and wanted to be with fun people my own age. We literally walked in and out within two minutes. The group of people in this meeting was so far gone that they could barely even breathe, let alone speak coherently. This was definitely not my crowd. I did not relate to anyone in the room, and I certainly did not aspire to anything they had.

Since I wanted Brendan more than I wanted to drink, I decided to give not drinking a try, on my own and without any help. For the next nine months, I did not drink or do any hard drugs, but still smoked pot. I considered myself to be sober. However, because I was still smoking pot, I was not really sober. Yet, I was less anesthetized than I had been for a very long time.

I white-knuckled through this period using willpower alone, and resented every minute of it. I was seething with rage all the time, and had no clue as to how to deal with my feelings. Being trapped in my own skin, twenty-four hours a day, without anesthesia was excruciating. Smoking pot was not enough. It was torture to go to work every day at Horizon and serve drinks. I watched everyone around me get drunk, yet could not take a drink myself. There was no longer anything to take the edge off. This was not fair. I felt like a caged animal. How could people possibly go through life without the relief of a drink? I could not stand being with myself anymore. I was angry all the time, and I really, really wanted a drink.

I hung on by my fingernails. After about nine months, I started to develop a crush on a customer at the bar, an avant-garde artist from New York, named Tom. Although I was Brendan's girlfriend, and Brendan was now working as the doorman at Horizon, I could not stop thinking about

Tom. He was at the bar regularly, and so was Brendan. I was developing an uneasiness that I could not handle. I knew I was coming to a breaking point.

I wanted two incompatible things simultaneously. It was too difficult to not drink and also try to cope with my emotions. If I started drinking again, there would definitely be big problems with Brendan, but I would no longer be under his control. This would free me up to be able to drink again and also to have the opportunity to see where things might go with Tom. It was crazy, but it made sense at the time. In reality, I was just using my "feelings" about Tom as an excuse to drink again.

It was New Year's Eve, and I could not be a good girl for a moment longer. I decided to take my long-awaited drink—with Tom. I was home again. Nothing ever materialized with my relationship with Tom, but I did not care. I was reunited with my real love, alcohol. I had missed being able to drink, and now felt like myself again. Things with Brendan deteriorated after that. Although Brendan also started drinking and using drugs again, we could no longer make it work. We continued to work together at Horizon, but went our separate ways.

As is true in recovery, the addiction progresses even if you are not using or drinking. Although I had a nine month period without alcohol, I was much worse off when I started drinking again. This time, I lost control of myself at an even deeper level. The same was true for Brendan. Both of us got deeper into our addictions, and went further down the scale than we had even gone before. I started drinking more than ever and doing as many drugs as I could get my hands on. A short time later, Brendan had a serious accident on his BMW motorcycle while under the influence, and was badly hurt. He survived, but spent many months on crutches.

The clientele at Horizon was very diverse, and included drug dealers who knew that we were raking in the money. We bartenders were easy prey for the dealers to cultivate as regular customers. One of the dealers, Michael, was the first to approach me. I had met him years before at Tiffany's, and knew him from the downtown scene. One night, he offered me some free drugs: a small bag of heroin. I took it, remembering how much I had loved it years ago when I had accidentally tried it with Scott when I was in college. I snorted it that night with one of the customers from the bar. We went to my house, and he said to me,

"Watch out for this stuff. It is very seductive."

"What do you mean?" I said.

"It sneaks up on you, and you don't even know it. If you're not careful, you won't be able to leave it alone."

"I won't have that problem," I reassured him. "I know what I'm doing."

As it turns out, he was right. I continued to use it for a while, but slowly realized that I could not stay away from it. When I first started using heroin, I was careful to space out several days between each use. Slowly, I used it more often. I was snorting it, and getting high just fine. Eventually, my tolerance went up, and I was not getting the same high I used to get. I needed more of it to get the same high. I knew I was getting in deeper, and there was nothing I could do to stop it. I was also drinking heavily and using everything else I could get my hands on. Drugs and alcohol were taking over my psyche and my existence. I was constantly preoccupied with the next high.

It was at this point that drugs and alcohol became more important than everything else in my life, even relationships. I no longer cared whether I had a boyfriend. I had no interest in anyone with whom I could not use drugs or alcohol, and was completely cut off from myself and everyone who loved me. I had finished my undergraduate studies at Hopkins, and had no plans for the future, except to stay high. I was using several times a week, and I was still trying to tell myself that I was not hooked.

I rationalized my decision not to proceed with my education or career by telling myself that I "needed a break." I had no interest in the future or in building a life for myself. I went to great lengths to hide my heroin use, so that no one really knew what was going on. Every day, I put on a mask for the world. There was the person I wanted you to think I was, and then there was the person I really was.

Opiates were different from other drugs I had done. They captured my spirit in a way that was all-encompassing. I desired the sweet, dark anesthesia from a place deep within my being. I wanted to be with other people who were doing the same thing. There was nothing more erotic than getting high with someone and then being sexual together for hours on end. I was flying solo, meeting new people, and having late-night adventures after the bar closed.

I started noticing a guy in the bar, Colin. I suspected that he was also doing heroin. I could tell just by looking at him. He looked very English, like a rock star. He had light blue eyes, and when he was high, the pupils of his eyes had that obvious and unmistakable opiate pinning. This attracted me to him, because I wanted to get closer to the drug. Once I got to know him, I discovered that I was right. He was, in fact, a well-seasoned heroin user. He had just moved to town from New York, and had lots of good drug connections up there. We often went to Alphabet City on the lower east side of New York on my days off just to score. The dope there was very cheap and also high quality. The scene was very seedy, but at the time, I thought it was cool.

In Baltimore, heroin was harder to get, and although I was still snorting it, I was continuing to develop a higher and higher tolerance. It was taking more and more to achieve the same high. Fortunately, I had plenty of money, so I could afford as much as I wanted. The bar was hopping most nights of the week, and the cash flowed. Although I usually spent all of my money, I never got into debt. So I told myself with delusion and pride that I was being financially responsible.

I was living with my father, who did not charge me any rent, so I could spend everything I made on drugs. He did not keep tabs on me, and allowed me to do whatever I wanted. He was in the bloom of his law career, and was also very involved in political activities after work. Since he was gone most of the time, he did not see a lot of what was going on. We sometimes hung out together at home, but we both had our own separate lives.

I started to spend more and more time with Colin, and eventually my heroin consumption progressed to intravenous use. I had never wanted to do this, but as my tolerance kept rising, I had no other choice. Snorting did not cut it anymore. I was compelled to either get high or go into physical withdrawal. At the time, it was a no-brainer.

Shooting heroin required assistance, because I physically could not perform the act by myself. Each time I did it, I needed Colin or someone else to help me. Colin needed me too for different reasons. He had lost his job installing alarm systems, and was now without money or a place to live. I suggested he temporarily come and stay with me at my father's apartment, which he periodically did.

Eventually, I lost my bartending job at Horizon. I was fired for hosting an unauthorized birthday party in the club after hours. I had gotten on the wrong side of Mildred, the long-time American Indian majority owner, and there was no way to salvage the situation. I was removed from the throne at Horizon, and was completely at a loss as to what to do next. My entire identity had been wrapped around being the bartender at the hottest spot in downtown Baltimore. I did not know who I was outside of the bar, and I did not want to give up my status. But there was no choice in the matter.

Out of desperation, I quickly moved on to another, but less desirable bartending job at The Outer Zone. This was a bar around the corner from Horizon that was trying to make it, but had never really taken off. I worked there for a couple of months; however it was not the same thing. It eventually became clear that I was no longer meant to work in the bar business. The party was over. This was a blessing in disguise.

I then decided to try life in the professional world. I got a job working at my father's law firm as his paralegal and office manager. I had no experience, but I was able to learn on the job. My father was carrying my load 100%. He loved me deeply, and wanted to give me a chance to learn some new skills in order to do something of value with my life. Although it was an enormous struggle to get up in the morning and have to medicate myself with enough heroin to get through the day, it also felt respectable to get dressed up and go to an office. It was time to try to grow up and become part of the real world.

I very much admired my father for having gone back to law school at the age of thirty-six to become an attorney and subsequently start his own law firm in his forties. I was very fortunate to have had this type of role model in my life. It took courage, commitment, and determination on his part. He showed me that anything was possible if I took action towards my goals. It was never too late. Because he had started his law career late in life, I felt that I too had time to find my way. I would know what to do when the time was right.

During my year at the law firm I regularly went out drinking after work with Katie, one of the other paralegals. We generally went to happy hours around five o'clock and kept drinking until eight or nine. By then, we were really drunk, and the cravings for drugs began. Getting coke or heroin would keep the night going. It was not uncommon for me to go to Horizon to find drinking and drugging companions so that the night did not have to end.

The chronic problem was that it was never possible to have a drink or two, say enough is enough, and go home and get to bed like other working people did. Regular people went out for happy hour. They could go home, have dinner, and go to bed and be able to get up for work the next morning. For me, this was next to impossible. Once I went out, I would stay out until there was no other choice. For an alcoholic or addict, it is difficult to put the brakes on.

After drinking for a few hours, the cocaine cravings took over, followed by the need to come down with some heroin or pills. One thing always led to another. Finding the drugs at odd hours was always a major ordeal, and it usually had to be done on a daily basis. This was a full-time job in and of itself. And to complicate matters, drug dealers are not very honest or reliable. Sometimes you would be in withdrawal, give someone money to get you some dope, and they would never come back. Other times, they would come back, but give you something that was low-quality or bogus. On good days, you did not get ripped off, the stuff was good, and there was somebody available to administer it. It was a lot of work.

One night after an extended happy hour, I was arrested for DWI. It was my first substance-related arrest. I lied my way through the court intake evaluation. By minimizing and misrepresenting my use of alcohol, it appeared as though the arrest had simply been bad luck during an aberration of conduct. I presented the image of a well-bred, good girl, which made my story more believable. This was easy to do, because I looked the part.

In court, I got off with probation before judgment. As long as there was no more trouble for the next year, the arrest would go away without any major repercussions. This had been a frightening experience, so I attempted to be more careful, which meant that I tried to cut back my drinking a little bit for a month or two. Eventually, the unpleasant memories faded and my complacency, arrogance, and recklessness returned. I was back up to my old tricks at full speed.

As time passed, Colin and I both got deeper into our addictions, and things got worse. My tolerance kept increasing. It got to the point where I was never getting high anymore. The next hit of heroin only kept me from going into withdrawal for a little while. My addiction had progressed to the point where I was in withdrawal sickness every day, and needed dope to be able to function or show up for anything at all. I needed something every morning and evening, or I could not operate. At one time, drugs were my slave, now they were my master.

6

ENSLAVED

I was a hostage of my addiction. I was trapped in a prison of my own making and could not find the key to escape. I knew that I had to change my life, but could not find my way out of the darkness. I tried to control my addiction, and kept failing. I told myself every day that if I was stronger, tried harder and was more determined, then I could overcome my obsessive thinking and compulsively self-destructive behavior. Every day I tried to stop, and every day I failed.

In the morning, I would tell myself that I was not going to use that day. By lunchtime, the cravings kicked in, and I was counting down the hours until happy hour. I told myself that I would have just one innocent drink to take the edge off. After that one drink, I was off to the races. I caved in, and promised myself to stop using tomorrow. When tomorrow came, the cycle started again. The tomorrows were never-ending.

Addiction is a disease of isolation, loneliness, and dishonesty. It is the only disease that tells you that you do not have a disease. Every day, I told myself that I was not going to use or drink, and every day I betrayed myself. I was desperate, miserable, and out of ideas. So I just kept doing the same thing over and over again, and expected different results. This is the definition of insanity.

As my frustration mounted, I was desperate to change something, so I changed jobs. I went to work as an export agent for a French and German international trading corporation at Baltimore's inner harbor. This was the first "real" job that I had gotten on my own, and I was very excited and proud. I was determined to be somebody, and to be respectable. I felt that if I could maintain this job, then I was alright. If I could keep the externals in place, then I was still on the right track. The best I could come up with was to try to look good on the outside, because I had not a clue as to how to change my insides. This was the most I could muster.

Around the same time, I also attempted to go to graduate school for the first time. I was accepted into a master's program at the University of Maryland in Intercultural Communication. This choice was made primarily because my godmother, Angela, was a professor in the department and I felt a connection there. I did not know what else to do. It also seemed like a program that could enhance my new career in international trade.

I was drifting along without direction or goals. I had no particular plan, other than to simply get a master's degree. I felt that in order to reach any professional status, I would need more than a college degree, even though my B.A. was from Johns Hopkins, an excellent university. My plan was to work during the day at the trading company, SRS International, and to attend graduate classes in the evenings.

This plan was unrealistic. I had not factored in the time required to maintain my addiction and recover from its effects. That, in and of itself, was more than a full-time job. Showing up at work was a daily challenge. It was a rare occasion that I could get to bed at an early enough hour to get a good night's sleep and be fresh for work in the morning. Even if I managed to stay in, I usually needed some heroin to avoid going into physical withdrawal and getting really physically sick. It was a full-time job just making sure I had enough drugs, enough money to keep buying more, and having Colin or someone else available to help me get the job done. I was trying to juggle too many things at once.

It was very difficult to curtail my nightlife, because if I went out for happy hour after work, it was too easy to end up in the bars all night long, and then fall prey to the compulsion to look for drugs by the end of the evening. This would invariably lead to staying up too late, usually alternating coke, heroin, and alcohol throughout the evening. Each substance led to a craving for the next substance, which would counteract the effects of the former. I wanted to be a responsible person, but my disease had control. I could not get off the merry-go-round.

It was always the first drink that was the problem. It was the first drink that led to everything else, but I could not see that reality. I tried to figure out exactly which drink was the problem. Was it the third, sixth, or eighth drink that made me lose control? I really wanted to know the answer to this question so that I could manage my drinking. I believed that if I could control my drinking, I could control everything else. The illusion that I could stop after just one drink persisted with remarkable stubbornness, and I continued to try to direct my own life. I failed every single day.

Throughout this year, I was doing poorly both at work and in school. I showed up at work most days, but not always. When I was able to show up for work, I was performing well below my potential. I had missed important deadlines and mismanaged some projects. I was rarely able to attend my graduate classes, and was overwhelmed by the work. After getting off of work, I had to choose between going to class and going to the bar. Most nights, I chose the bar.

Drinking gave me relief and escape. I wanted to want to deal with my responsibilities, but the truth was that I just wanted to medicate myself into numbness. The less I went to class, the harder it was to go the next time. I met each class day with shame, dread, and a sense of impending doom. I knew that I was so far behind that it would be impossible to catch up. I eventually gave up and withdrew at the end of the first semester.

I was starting to throw in the towel. I could not keep it together after all, and I was letting go. It was exhausting. Every day was a battle and a struggle to medicate myself as needed, and to try to make it through and show up for my commitments in the outside world. I would relish the days when I did not have to go anywhere, and I could just lie in bed all day, get high, and watch television. My dream was to be as close to comatose as possible, and have no responsibilities to attend to. My closest relationships were with television characters and game show hosts. I would isolate for long periods of time, either recovering from a binge or trying to get ready for another one.

One alternative to using street drugs was to purchase black-market methadone from my dealer. He was able to get it from other addicts who were on the methadone maintenance program. They sometimes did not need it or chose to use heroin that day instead of taking their daily take-home dose of methadone. I wanted to detoxify myself off of opiates, and this was recommended by my dealer as the magic potion that would make it possible. Drinking a measured portion of methadone could keep the withdrawal symptoms from occurring. By slowly decreasing the dose of methadone over several days, I repeatedly attempted to detoxify myself from heroin and overcome the physical withdrawal symptoms.

It became clear that getting off of drugs could not be done without some kind of help, but my current strategy was not working. Again, I was trying to control my addiction by myself, with more drugs. I would get down to the last orange liquid dose in the small bottle, and commit myself to the end of using. I swore that this was it. No more. I was going to stick with it this time. A day or two would go by, the methadone would wear off, and then the cravings for opiates would overtake me once again. The plan was never successful. After a few days, I always relapsed and sought out heroin.

The pull of the addiction was irresistible. Usually, the slip backwards would begin by getting together with Colin. I would "innocently" want to see him. Invariably, he would be using heroin, because he did not want to stop, and did not pretend that he did. It was always a matter of time after seeing him that we ended up using together. Just the sight of him made me want to get high. Then I would blame him for making me relapse. I was unconsciously making him the bad guy and using him as an excuse for my own addiction.

I had been kicking him out of my life intermittently when I was trying to clean up. I knew that I could not stay clean if I had any contact with him. He was always using, and had good connections to get more. I had money, so he was always glad to see me when I called and asked him to come back. It was very difficult to stay away from him because my addiction kept driving me back. Using drugs was and had always been the basis for our relationship. There was little actual genuine relationship under it all; we were mainly drug buddies who met each others' dependency needs in different ways.

Eventually I got fired from SRS International for poor performance and attendance problems. My boss was a very kind Frenchman named Claude, who did not confront me directly about my addiction, but indicated that he knew what was going on. He promised to give me a good reference, and sent me on my way. I felt humiliated, embarrassed and indignant. Deep down, however, I understood why I had been fired. At this point, I gave up on trying to make it all work.

For the first time, I had no pretense of a life that even resembled anything normal. I was so exhausted from trying to keep up the charade of a normal life, that I welcomed a break. I decided to just take the summer "off." I told myself that I was tired, and that I needed a break from all the years of working and being in school. What had really exhausted me, though, was my addiction. Being an addict is really hard work.

I was now a twenty-seven-year-old with no life plan, and was still living at my father's apartment. I decided to relax and focus on my favorite pastime, pleasure-seeking. It had been a very lazy, hazy summer, and I knew that I needed to do something with myself. I spent my days sleeping, shopping, hanging out with other unemployed friends, and waiting for the nights to come so that I could go out to the bars. We would go out at nine o'clock at night, stay out until the bars closed, find an after-hours hang out, and then do drugs until dawn. Someone always had drugs, and that would enable us to stay up as long as we wanted to.

The rising of the sun was always very depressing in those days, because it meant that the party was over—at least for that particular day. It also meant that you had to try to get to sleep, which was often very challenging after a night of paranoia-inducing stimulants and heroin. The best case scenario was being able to sleep all day and then get up again when the sun went down and start the cycle all over again.

I was tired of the scene in Baltimore, including my drug-using friends and the bar crowd. I wasted precious years of my life drinking and squandered a vast number of opportunities. I desperately needed structure and direction in my life, but felt completely lost and unable to ask for help. I was stuck, and could not get out. I could not envision a real life as a responsible person. I wanted out of the abyss, but I was trapped.

Drugs had taken over my life, and they now completely controlled me and all of my choices. Having a day job would interfere with my using and partying, so that was out of the question. I lived each day in order to use and to anesthetize myself. My ongoing goal was to be as numb as possible. On most days, I achieved my goal.

After getting fired from SRS, I spent all the money I had saved from my working days. The money to fund my lifestyle now came from taking cash advances from my credit cards. I had crossed another line that I had never envisioned crossing. I had previously always been a financially solvent person. I was now running up debt out of desperation, with no prospects for income on the horizon. My value system was eroding even more. How would I ever be able to stop using and pay off the debt? Deep down, I knew I was not the person I wanted to be. I knew I had lost control.

I grew up in the 60's and 70's era of anything-goes. It was cool to use drugs. I had idolized the counter-culture, rebels, rock stars, models and hippies. They were wild and lived life on the edge. This is what I thought living fully was about. I thought that being a sober person was boring; the equivalent of a living death. When I met straight people who did not party, they seemed like pathetic losers who never had any fun. I thought that they were missing out on life. What had previously seemed like a cool way of life was now turning into a bummer.

I did not want to merely exist; I wanted to really live. I believed that using drugs and having relationships with men was what living was really about. If I could get just the right high and the right guy, life would magically fall into place and I would live happily ever after. The high would make me feel good, and the guy would take care of me and meet all my needs. This mentality was not unlike that of an infant who wants to be fed by the mother's breast and cared for by an ever-present parent. This was my magical thinking. Unfortunately, the fantasy was giving way to reality.

I was starting to not have any fun anymore. Drugs and alcohol were turning on me, and there was no way to turn things back to the way they used to be. The party was ending. Using was no longer working. I tried to reverse the process, but there was nothing I could do to make drugs and alcohol provide the gratification for me that they once had. I continued to try to use, and it kept becoming increasingly painful. I needed more and more. Even when I did manage to actually get high, the high itself did not feel euphoric. It felt stale, numb, flat, and empty. I felt dead inside.

7
QUICKSAND

I wanted something different and new. I needed a new boyfriend, a new job, a new place to live, maybe even a new city. I could not stand myself anymore. What I really needed was a new me, but I was looking to change everything outside of myself instead. It was a lot easier to look outside than inside. Alcoholics and addicts will often go to great lengths to change everything around them in order to avoid looking at themselves and address their own issues. The problem is always another person, the job, the place, the family, or something else outside of themselves.

I eventually got the idea that it would be a good idea to apply to another graduate program. This time I chose a program in French literature at The Catholic University of America, in Washington, D.C. I did not have a career track, and the only thing I had really loved doing in school was studying and speaking French, which I had done well for fifteen years. I thought that perhaps I could parlay my love of French into something. Anything. I did not know what else to do. I was grasping at straws.

I had grown up with a love of France and everything French. This was the result of the influence of my godparents, Kishin and Angela, who are both Francophiles. They always had a deep affiliation with France, which they had imparted to me throughout my life. They had homes in Paris and Baltimore, and had successfully integrated France into their American lives. Since birth, they had had an enormous influence on my life and psyche. Angela was a French professor of German origin; Kishin was a physicist from India. They were both very sophisticated people with world-class taste and refinement. They did not have their own children, so I became their surrogate child. They were very close to me and my parents in my early years. I still consider them my "other parents."

On one of my trips to Paris, I made a friend named Cathy, who had gotten her master's degree in Italian at Catholic University and had raved about their foreign language department. This also made Catholic University seem like a good choice. I was accepted into the master's program in French literature in the fall of 1989. This meant that I would be taking graduate-level classes, as well as teaching a few undergraduate-level classes in French grammar in order to fulfill the fellowship requirements and receive a monthly stipend.

I was relieved at finally having respectable future plans. It was very important to me that I be able to tell people that I was doing something of value. Inside, I knew I was not progressing in my life, and I did not feel any sense of self-worth. I desperately needed something to make me feel better about myself.

The plan of living in Baltimore, waking up early to get to the train station to catch the commuter train to Washington, D.C., and then reaching Catholic University in time to teach undergraduate classes was overly-optimistic. It was difficult enough just to wake up at all in the morning, let alone getting myself to Washington, D.C. Due to my addiction and alcoholism, it was difficult for me to show up where I was supposed to be, even locally in Baltimore.

I had the best of intentions, but it was practically impossible to carry them out to fruition. I was in over my head. I gave it an honest attempt, but it was far too ambitious for my current state of health. I knew that my life was out of control, and I was trying to prove to myself that I could function as a normal person. I once again felt that if I could keep things looking good on the outside, then I was still okay.

I had first admitted to myself that I was an alcoholic at age eighteen, when my then-boyfriend, Scott, pointed it out to me after a very disturbing night of blackout drinking which culminated in my wandering off and disappearing until the next morning. Prior to this incident, I knew I was using drugs and alcohol heavily, but thought I could control my use. I also believed that I could stop if I wanted to, but that there was nothing that would ever make me want to. Now, years later, I had had many more blackouts, all-night binges, and negative consequences from using, It was clearly getting worse all the time.

I continued to try different approaches to controlling my using. Maybe if I did some opiates, less pot, more alcohol and less coke, I could manage things better. Or perhaps I needed to stop opiates and only smoke pot and drink socially. The combinations were endless. I was like a mad scientist trying to figure out the right combination of drugs and alcohol that I could manage successfully. It had never occurred to me that I could not handle any of it. It was like switching seats on the Titanic.

I started in the graduate program at Catholic University in the fall if 1989. On the second day, I missed the Marc commuter train coming back to Baltimore by two minutes. I was exasperated, and did not know what to do with myself until the next train. It was the end of the day, and I was tired, weak and starting to not feel well from heroin withdrawal. I had managed to get through the first two days by using just enough heroin to not be in withdrawal during the day, but not so much that I was high. I was trying to use every approach I could think of to clean up and straighten myself out.

I walked through Washington's Union station and saw the sun coming in through the large beautiful windows. It was late afternoon and the light was stunning. Out of the knife store in the shopping arcade emerged my old friend from Hopkins, Alex. I was astonished to run into him. He looked amazing. With his long blond hair and tall, tan physique, he was a bewildering sight for my eyes.

I had not seen Alex for several years. We had been drug buddies and occasional lovers during my first couple of years in college. While at Hopkins, he had a multitude of car accidents while under the influence of opiates and had suffered multiple long-term serious injuries. He had withdrawn from Hopkins after being arrested for fraudulent prescription charges, and then had to spend time in jail.

After everything that had happened to him, I had not known if he was in jail, or if he was even still alive.

Alex was a brilliant man who used his misguided genius to master the DEA code and then pose as various fictitious doctors in order to prescribe opiate medications for himself. He had a lengthy roster of fraudulent medical identities, as well as bogus patients. He had been arrested for prescription fraud seventeen times, but somehow managed to stay out of jail most of the time and eventually land on his feet. Each time he started over, he put together another fabulous life; until he sabotaged it again. This time, Alex was living in Washington, D.C. and was working as a French cheese expert at a gourmet market in Dupont Circle.

As soon as I saw him, I immediately knew that Alex was high. He had a familiar stoned look in his eyes and the detached air of someone who was chemically fortified. I could tell by his demeanor that he might have access to something that would take the edge off my withdrawal. Maybe I could get some drugs from him, I thought.

We talked for a while, and I asked him if he could help me out. He said he could, and also asked me if I wanted to stay with him in D.C. that night. That seemed like a fine idea. I really did not have anything better to do, and it might be a fun adventure. I did not have any extra clothes with me, so I went to a store in Union Station and bought an outfit for the next day. I had to be back at Catholic to teach early in the morning, so it was essential to show up looking fresh and professional. We drank codeine cough syrup, stayed up all night, and renewed our romantic relationship.

After that night, I went back to Baltimore a couple of times, but soon shifted to staying at Alex's apartment in Glover Park. It was wonderful to be in a new environment and in a new city. Now that I was with Alex, there was no further need for heroin or street drug dealers. I was able to readily obtain codeine cough syrup and pills from him in order to keep the opiate withdrawal at bay. This somehow felt more legitimate and respectable than buying street drugs from sleazy dealers. I was now taking mostly prescription medications, and felt like I was clean in comparison to what I had been doing in Baltimore.

It turned out to be a very positive decision to get out of Baltimore and away from the old crowd. Washington was a fresh environment, and I did not have all of the drinking and drugging memories and connections that were ubiquitous in Baltimore. Everything that I saw, touched, and remembered in Baltimore was about partying and using. The toxic memories overshadowed any healthy ones by far. In Washington, there were no external triggers that could lead me back to my old haunts. There were, however lots of internal triggers that I still had to contend with. I still had to deal with me, but it seemed much more possible in a new place.

Throughout the fall, I continued to struggle with my opiate addiction. There was no longer any high. As tolerance goes up, it becomes harder and harder to achieve the same high. Every day, the goal was to not be sick from withdrawal and to try make it through the workday. Alex supplied the pills through his fraudulent prescriptions, and we were keeping ourselves afloat financially.

I spent most of my free time living my dream—lying in bed, smoking pot, watching television and zoning out. This time, however, the dream had morphed into a nightmare. I felt awful all the time, and I did not have any energy to live life. Nothing kills drive energy quite the way that marijuana does. When you smoke it, you are quite content to just do nothing and marvel at the thoughts in your head. Then afterwards, you cannot remember a thing.

I was showing up for my teaching commitments at Catholic University, but was not keeping up with my own master's program. It was too much work. After an exam on Thanksgiving eve 1989, I realized that I was probably not going to pass the semester, and I panicked. There was no way to go back in time and undo what had been blown over the past several months. Just as I had done in college, I had not shown up for my classes. However, at the graduate level, this was irreparable. I had missed too much. There was no way to catch up, recover and pass the class.

Like any good alcoholic, the only solution that came to mind was to go out and get really drunk. No matter what the problem, issue, or celebration was about, the solution was always to ingest a chemical. With addiction, however, the "solution" eventually becomes the problem. On the way home from Catholic, I stopped at a bar in Adams Morgan.

I started doing tequila shots straight up with lemon, and the last thing I remember was sitting at the bar. I remember the hazy blur of the restaurant area, which slowly went out of focus over the first hour. There had not been many people there, as it was fairly early in the afternoon. The next vague memory of that evening was much later when I was driving in the snow, lost, and trying to find my way home. The rest of the evening was a complete blackout.

The next day, I came out of my blackout in a police station in Washington D.C. I was screaming at the police to let me out of my cell. I had been robbed, had no purse or identification, and was convinced that the police had stolen my belongings. I was so sure that the police were the culprits in this situation that I had no hesitation about berating them for it. Fortunately, the police tolerated my insanity without enforcing further repercussions. Shortly thereafter, Alex appeared at the police station and bailed me out. We went home and I lived under an even darker cloud of horror and shame that would not budge easily.

Since this was my second DWI, it was a much more serious matter. Getting off the first time with probation was a gift, but this time it was going to be different. One possible outcome was time in jail. There was no question that second-time DWI offenders were treated more harshly. The terror of the consequences of this second arrest was life-changing. My denial was penetrated, and it was clear that I was destroying my future at the age of twenty-seven.

I knew beyond any doubt that I would soon have to completely change my life and give up all drugs and alcohol. This second arrest was the proof that I needed to demonstrate that I could not manage my own life. Nothing I had tried was working, and everything just kept getting worse. I knew that if I continued to use drugs and alcohol, my life was only going to continue to deteriorate further. Whatever was going to happen would certainly be unbearable. There was no longer any way to blame all of this on bad luck. I was slowly giving up, but this process would still take several months, even after the arrest.

On New Year's Eve 1990, Alex and I went to Baltimore to celebrate the New Year. We really let it rip. We had just gotten engaged to be married and were committed to making a life together. For the holiday, we were determined to really celebrate. We wanted to have extra fun. We wanted to go beyond the daily norm of simply maintaining our chemical balance in order to avoid withdrawal. This meant getting higher than usual. After stocking up on pills and cough syrup, we went out to the clubs in Baltimore to find my old crowd. The evening was a blur of old friends, bars and drinking. At the end of the evening, we found some heroin and added it to the mix.

I was completely nonfunctional for the next five days, and could not even get out of bed until January 5th. Those first days of 1990 were the darkest days I had ever seen. Never before had I been so ill for so long from using drugs and alcohol. This was the most painful hangover ever. Upon re-emerging into the world, a new awareness became apparent that nothing was fun anymore. I had to be not only unhappy, but really, really miserable for a very long time to realize that I was not having fun anymore.

8

OUT OF THE WOMB

The abyss of addiction was ever-deepening and all-consuming to the point of utter exhaustion. After grieving November's arrest and feeling sorry for myself for the next couple of months, I finally came to the moment of clarity that led to getting sober. I had been continuing to spend the majority of my time, outside of teaching at Catholic University, in bed at Alex's apartment.

The loneliness and vastness of the emptiness of my life were inescapable. There was nothing that could fill me up anymore. No drugs. No alcohol. No guy. No new place. No job. No nothing. It was the season of death-freezing, God-awful, desolate February, which only made matters worse. I felt progressively more barren inside, and nothing could make the painful feelings go away. I finally got to the point where the pain was greater than my resistance to change. I became willing to reach out for help.

Once I admitted to myself that I could not do it alone, I surrendered inside. I knew that I could not live this way anymore. I had tried for a long time, and it just was not workable. The first call that I made was to my father. I felt very safe with him, because he had never judged or criticized me. I hoped that he would be supportive of what I was about to say. I called him and said:

"Daddy, I need to talk to you about something really important."

He said, "What is it Aniti?"

I said, "I have an addiction problem and I really need help."

He said, "Well, I'm glad you're dealing with this, and I'll do whatever I can to help you."

There was warmth, love, and understanding in his voice. He had seen me struggle for many years, and already knew what I had just told him. He also understood addiction on a personal level, because he had had his own struggles. He responded with such tenderness and unconditional acceptance that I felt safe enough to be vulnerable and to express myself honestly for the first time ever.

The next step was to talk to my mother. I feared doing this, because she was more authoritative and parental than my father. I had lied to her more and avoided her throughout my entire life. Bringing out the truth to her was serious business. To my surprise, when I opened up to her honestly about my addiction, she was equally accepting and loving. Alex and I then went to Baltimore to meet with her to discuss a plan for getting clean.

I decided to write out a new detoxification schedule to wean myself off of Tylenol with codeine. This was the last addiction that I still had to overcome, but it was a step down from where I had been before. I thought I could get off of the pills by systematically reducing the dosage by small increments every few days, and eventually getting down to zero. I hypothesized that the more slowly I went down, the less painful the detoxification would be.

I wanted to get off of the pills with as little physical difficulty as possible, in order to minimize the chance of relapse. I had to be able to function during the day, because I was still teaching French at Catholic University. I knew that if the withdrawal was too harsh, I would cave in and start using more drugs. By decreasing the dosage by one half, and then subsequently one quarter grain per day, I could monitor the decrease very closely and then hopefully become liberated from the pills.

The nice thing about the pills was that they could be managed more easily than street drugs. The quality and dosage were laboratory-controlled, which took the guesswork out of exactly what was going in my body. Ironically, I was also quite concerned about contaminating my system with unnecessary Tylenol. In order to minimize the amount of Tylenol going into my system, I crushed up the pills and then dissolved them in water. The Tylenol would sink to the bottom and separate from the water, which was then became a clear codeine solution. It was then possible to remove the liquid solution from the Tylenol, leaving only the codeine in water, which could be easily portioned out in measured doses.

I had tried to implement this system for the past several months, complete with a written daily schedule, but had failed repeatedly. Time and time again, I would start out with good intentions, but relapse back to using large amounts of pills and cough syrup in order to try to get really high again. This would set me back quite a bit. The next time I began another detox, I would have to begin at a very high dosage level, and gradually work my way down to where I had started before. It was a never-ending roller-coaster.

Even though I was not given an immediate resolution to my addiction, the very act of admitting my problem and reaching out to people in honesty set me on a new path. From this point on, I continued to seek help, and spoke to any and everyone whom I thought might be able to be of assistance. I had broken out of my prison. I was no longer alone with my addiction. Once I put the truth out to the universe, it became a reality that had to be dealt with. This small act set into motion a series of events which would conspire to help and guide me toward what I needed. This was the beginning of a new way of life.

Alex was also trying to get off drugs, and was experiencing the same cycle of relapse. This happened countless times. The problem was that between the two of us, one of us was always caving in and getting off track. This would then pull the other person down. I would try to be good for a while, but then he would want to get high, and I could not stop myself from joining him. At other times, it was the reverse. We were joined by our addictions, and colluded in the relationship to remain ill. This time, however, one thing was different.

Alex said, "I know how we can do this."

"What do you mean?" I said.

"We need to go to meetings."

"What meetings? What are you talking about?"

"There are these meetings that we can go to in George-town. The people there are alcoholics and addicts, just like us. There are a lot of interesting people who are young and cool. They are all trying to stop using."

"What do they do there?"

"They just get together and talk about life."

"When can we go?"

"There is a meeting on Thursday night at 8:30. But it's a men's meeting, so you'll have to dress a little boyish, okay?"

"Okay," I said. I was desperate enough to give anything a try at this point. I was determined to get off the merry-go-round. I had tried and failed on my own too many times. I knew that I needed to do something differently. If this was working for other people, maybe it could work for me too. I wanted find out what it was all about. Even if it meant try-ing to pass myself off as a guy.

The following Thursday, I got dressed up in baggy clothes and no makeup. I tucked my waist-length hair into a big cowboy hat, and tried to look like a boy. We stopped in the local drugstore and Alex got us a bottle of codeine cough syrup. We each guzzled down half of the bottle, and then went across the street to the recovery meeting.

The meeting was held at the Westside Club, which was located on the second floor of a building in Georgetown. As we entered the club, we had to pass through a room where a coed meeting was taking place in order to get to the men's meeting that Alex knew about. As we walked through the crowd in the first room, I noticed that the peo-ple there were young, good-looking, and happy. There were at least fifty people in the first room. This was a popular thing. They seemed happy to be together, and there was a warm feeling in the room.

We sheepishly entered the men's meeting, where the entire crowd of about thirty men all turned around and looked at us with curiosity as we came in late. A few minutes later, one of the men looked at me and said, "This is a men's meeting!" I did not flinch. Having just downed half a bottle of cough syrup, I was slightly more courageous and arrogant than usual. I just sat there and pretended that I was a guy.

Alex got really high from the cough syrup, but I did not. My tolerance was too high. Alex started to nod off in the meeting. I then became really embarrassed that he was nodding off, and that I was dressed in drag. We were a couple of conspicuous oddballs. I felt like an outcast that did not belong anywhere or with anyone. The truth was that I was jealous and furious with Alex for being able to get high, while I could not. If I had gotten high, I would not have cared about anything. We tried to stay for most of the meeting, but I became so irritated that I could barely sit still towards the end.

We left the meeting and went back to Alex's apartment in Glover Park. On the way home, I felt miserable and defeated. This did not feel as though it had gone well. What an outlandish fiasco. As we were getting out of the car, there was a guy getting out of his car a few yards away. He had been at the recovery meeting in Georgetown and recognized us.

He looked at me and said, "What you did was great. I hope you'll come back." He said this to me with delight, gusto and conviction. This small comment immediately lifted my anger, disgust, shame and discomfort about what had just happened. I no longer felt like a leper. I felt accepted and welcomed. This guy had actually gotten a kick out of what I had done! If there were people like this at these meetings, I wanted to know them. They were as fun-loving and crazy as I was. His comment made me feel comfortable about going back to another meeting, which I soon did.

I started going to co-ed meetings on a daily basis, and was able to stick to my detoxification schedule from Tylenol with codeine for the first time ever. Although I was not yet fully clean and sober, it was perfectly acceptable to go to the meetings anyway. The only requirement to attend the meetings was a desire to be sober; you did not actually have to already be sober. There was something that happened to me from going to the meetings that was different from anything that I had ever experienced before.

I was no longer alone with myself and my problems. I had support from people who were exactly like me. They started to get to know me, and regularly asked about my situation and how I was doing. They went out of their way to help me with every issue I faced. All I had to do was show up and talk about what was going on. I began to tap into the protective wall of the human community. This shielded me from the disease of addiction enough that I was able to escape my prison. Even though I still wanted to use, somehow I was given the power not to.

I had wanted to enjoy my life for a long time, but was unable to do so because of my addiction. I had been trapped, because I did not know there was another way to live. I had envisioned a life without drugs and alcohol to be very dull and confining. This was not what I saw at the meetings. It was just the opposite. I was really surprised.

The people in the meetings were very attractive to me, because they were happy, self-confident, and had a clear sense of who they were. They were enjoying their lives, and I wanted to know how they did it. I wanted what they had. They were living exciting, abundant lives, fueled by their own innate energy and sense of direction. They felt good about themselves, and were having a lot of fun.

This was what I had been in search of throughout my entire life. I had sought this from drugs and alcohol, but had never really found what I was looking for. As it turns out, it was actually the drugs and alcohol that were standing in the way of my actually getting what I wanted. Now, by giving up the drugs and alcohol, I could really have what I had wanted all along. How ironic.

I had to see it for myself to believe it. In meetings, it was possible to witness other sober people living their lives and sharing their innermost thoughts, experiences, and feelings about living without drugs and alcohol. They shared solutions to everyday life situations that had previously baffled to me. For example, how do you deal with being triggered to want to use because you are hungry? Eat a meal. How do you deal with being tired? Get some rest. What about when you get angry? Talk it out with someone. How do you keep yourself from going to happy hour after work? The solution was to go to a meeting instead. The program was a healthy substitute for drinking and drugging. You could work your program exactly the same way you drank.

The environment in the group was very honest and open. People spoke about themselves in a way that I had never experienced before. They were genuine, and they spoke from the heart. The environment was intimate, caring, and a lot of fun. There was a lot of laughter. It was also full of social interaction, which I desperately needed in my lonely, isolated life. It was so attractive that I wanted more and more. So I continued to go back.

An additional benefit of going to the meetings was that I got an attendance sheet signed at every meeting in preparation for my DWI case. I wanted the judge to know that I was serious about getting well. I was terrified about court, but was moving forward in faith. I thought that being in a recovery program would help my court situation, which it did. When the time finally came to go to court, I got sentenced to be on probation for one year, pay a small fine, and attend some alcohol education classes. This was relatively easy to deal with.

During the last days of the detoxification process, I still smoked pot and drank occasionally, but knew that these days were numbered. I had one final night out, which resulted in an immediate blackout, and an exceedingly remorseful next day. This was a blessing in disguise. It was on that day that I reached out for even more help and found a mentor in the recovery group. I called her every day to tell her how I was doing, and our connection was my lifeline to a new way of living. She was the missing piece that I had needed to anchor me to a new existence. The more help I sought, the better things got.

March 5, 1990 was my sobriety date. From that day onward, I would be completely off of alcohol and drugs, and begin my new life of total abstinence from all substances. This would mean no more liquefied codeine doses, valium, alcohol, pot, or anything else that was mood-altering. What a terrifying thought; nothing to lean on to take the edge off of reality. I really did not know if I could do this. What if I fell apart or went crazy? It was frightening, but living as I had been living was even more terrifying. With my newfound help, I summoned up enough courage to carry out and stick with my plan. One day at a time.

I had learned in the meetings that you could tackle anything one day at a time. By breaking down the issue to simply dealing with what was in front of me today, or even just this hour, it was possible to accomplish a previously insurmountable task, like not using when I had the urge. I could always drink or use tomorrow, I told myself, but I would not do it today. When tomorrow came, it became the new today, and the same principle of delay applied again. Usually, I was able to figure out a support plan that would carry me through until the end of the day. When I could not do it by myself, I could call someone and ask for help.

One of the keys to recovery was to cultivate a broad support system, and to stop going through life unarmed and alone. No matter what the situation, there was always someone in recovery who had been there before. If I had a particularly difficult event coming up, I learned to "book-end." This meant calling someone for support both before and after the event. In this way, I did not have to go through it all by myself.

The problem, I learned, was my own thinking. It was not the alcohol or drugs themselves, but my inherent thought processes and impaired decision-making abilities. Trying to make choices and decisions by myself, with only my own toxic brain to draw upon, had been a liability. That was the reason why I could not take constructive action that was in my own best interest in the past. When you are alone with your addiction, you are asking a toxic organ (your brain) to make rational decisions to try to fix itself and heal the disease. You cannot ask what is wrong with you to fix what is wrong with you. It is inherently impossible. Therefore, other people and outside help are essential for the recovery process.

The first few days were okay. I was a little shaky, but got through them. I did not feel well, but I was able to stay clean. Alex was supposedly getting sober along with me. He and I both knew that if we both did not do it at the same time, it could not work for either one of us. The using person would pull the other one back into our old ways. It had to be both of us with two feet in recovery, or neither one. On my fourth day of sobriety, March 9th, 1990, I was faced with a major challenge.

Alex had not come home that night. This was very unusual for Alex, so I knew that something serious had happened. He was not the type to have an affair, but he was the type to use drugs behind my back. I suspected that he had been arrested or was in the hospital, and started calling around to try to locate him. I panicked and was terrified. I knew something had gone terribly wrong. It turned out that he was arrested for prescription fraud, yet again, and had been detained in jail.

This point brought me to a very difficult choice. I had to choose between myself and Alex. I knew that if I stayed with Alex, I would be at serious risk of relapsing, because he was not ready to stop using. I knew that I was not strong enough to handle being around him. Even though I had made progress, it was going to be next to impossible to withstand the temptation of using while living with another active addict.

Not only was I addicted to drugs, but I was also addicted to Alex. He was at the center of my internal world. How was I going to be able go on without him? Would I be able to make it? Fortunately, my dependency on him was weakened by my newfound participation in the recovery meetings and the new relationships that were being forged there. I was developing a new dimension in my life with other people in recovery, which kept me from being so reliant upon Alex to meet my emotional needs.

The decision was made before Alex returned home. I called a few people to talk about the situation, and made my choice. I was leaving. There was no other option. I simply had to choose my own life over this unhealthy relationship. I had only come the short distance of four days in my recovery, but I had come too far to turn back now. It had taken so much to get through the detoxification in order to even get to my first day of total sobriety that I was unwilling to give up what I had accomplished. It had been achieved through enormous commitment, pain, and courage. I decided that it was not worth giving myself up for Alex. Sometimes you have to leave someone you love in order to survive.

I had nowhere to live, and did not want to return to Baltimore, as that was surely a dangerous and triggering environment for my addiction. Amazingly, I was able to make immediate arrangements to rent a room in the home of Marci, a friend from my recovery group. She was a public relations executive who owned a mansion in Foxhall, a beautiful neighborhood in Washington. She was single, lonely, and only too happy to rent out a room in order to have some company.

Moving at the speed of light, I packed up all my belongings and stuffed them into my Toyota. Within hours, I was living in a better place, and with another sober person. I had escaped the threat of being pulled back into my addiction at a crucial point in time. I knew that I was not strong enough to be with Alex any longer. He was nowhere near ready to stop using drugs, and there was no choice but to move on without him. Leaving was the only solution. Although it was extremely painful to leave him, it was more painful to stay.

Now at Marci's house, my new life began. The initial days were completely terrifying. My mood swings were severe and frequent. The physical rollercoaster was devastating. Waves of anxiety, blood sugar problems, depression, fatigue, and emotional outbursts would overtake me. My body, mind, and spirit were all in chaos, and were struggling to find equilibrium.

The only thing that I could hang on to was my recovery group. Through this group, I met many new friends. I started to build a life with healthy, sober people. They carried me emotionally as I walked through the fire. We would often talk and socialize before and after the meetings, which was just as important as attending the meetings themselves. I went to a meeting every day, sometimes more than once. Every time I went to a meeting, I felt better. I was somehow able to cope with whatever was going on, without finding it necessary to take a drink or a drug. I started having fun and enjoying my life. I was learning how to life for the first time ever.

9

BABY STEPS

The last semester of teaching at Catholic University was coming to a close, and it was time to make a decision about what to do next. Because the first order of business was to stay sober, I decided to put the primary focus on my recovery and just get any job that would pay the bills. Through an ad in the newspaper, I found my first job in sobriety working in the front office of the Watergate Hotel. I had never worked in this industry before, but had previously worked in a service capacity as a waitress and bartender.

What drew me to the ad was the fact that they were seeking someone who spoke French. At least I would be able to use my language skills, I thought. The Watergate had a very exclusive and international clientele, and all employees who interacted with guests were required to speak a second language in addition to English. I soon found myself in a work situation which I found to be very stressful. I was standing on my feet all day long. The hours were erratic. One day you were scheduled to work from seven in the morning until three-thirty in the afternoon. The next day, you might have to work from three o'clock in the afternoon until eleven-thirty at night. Then, the following day, you might have to work at seven o'clock in the morning again. Thus, in addition to being on the roller-coaster of early sobriety, the fluctuating schedule made it even more difficult to regulate my sleep cycle and achieve physical balance and emotional equilibrium.

Another challenge was in interacting with the guests. Because the Watergate catered to an exclusive clientele, there was a constant flow of celebrities and VIPs who came to stay there. They were sometimes wonderful to deal with, but at other times, extremely demanding and downright abusive. When they were unpleasant, we were required to respond with Teflon-like detachment and politeness. I was just learning how to function as a human being without drugs and alcohol, and was barely able to hold it together every day. I did not yet possess the skills to handle this crowd. I went in to work daily and tried to fake it. I pasted a big smile on my face, and tried to just deal with situations as appropriately as I could, as they came up.

Some days were better than others. I really needed the job because I had bills to pay. I was willing to do whatever it took, and bear any necessary hardship in order to make it on my own. No way was I going to go back to Baltimore. I had to tough it out. Even though I felt that the job was beneath me, I did not know what else to do. Every day, I felt like I was pretending to be a regular person, because I felt a lack of internal cohesiveness. Everybody else seemed normal and together. I felt like a defective person who was not good enough.

This was the exact feeling that I had as a child before I ever started using drugs and alcohol in the first place. My early experience was that I felt lost, confused, and had experienced shattering alienation throughout my entire life. Even before I ever took my first drink or drug, I was overcome by my chronic feelings of aloneness, and had never felt a part of anything.

Thus, when I got sober, all of these old feelings were right there waiting for me. However, they were intensified, because over the years, I had accumulated layers upon layers of unprocessed feelings. I had so much undigested emotional material that I was in a perpetual state of fragmented emotional confusion. This illustrates the fact that you cannot avoid dealing with whatever is trapped inside of you. There is no amount of drugs or alcohol that will ever really take the feelings away. Using substances will only delay the inevitable. Eventually, you must face yourself.

I felt as though drugs and alcohol had been the glue that had held me together. Without them, I was in a million pieces inside. I had no coping skills to deal with all the feelings associated with early recovery and post-acute withdrawal. I had spent my entire life trying to control and avoid my feelings. Now they were all there and I had to feel them. This was a really rude awakening.

I had also used drugs and alcohol to alleviate an enormous amount of social anxiety and depression throughout my life. Now there was no way to avoid those feelings; the only way through them was to simply experience them, and try to hang in there until I could get to the other side. Eventually, I always got there. Every bad feeling and difficult day ultimately passed. On most days for the first eighteen months, I felt crazy. Going to meetings daily allowed me to get through each day without returning to drugs and alcohol.

The power of self-help groups and recovery meetings can never be fully explained and understood, but they work. Meetings provide the same things that you tried to find in alcohol and drugs, but could not. The benefits of meetings are vast. They regulate affect states, reduce shame and build social supports. They provide a source of internal and external structure, as well as self-regulation, so that you can develop a cohesive sense of self. There are also physiological changes that occur in the brain as the result of meeting attendance. Many people report that their depression and anxiety lessens as a result of participation in self-help programs.

Emotional refueling occurs when a child goes to sit on the mother's lap and is held. Soothed by the mother's love and re-energized by her presence, the child is then able to go back out into the world, explore, and live away from the mother. After a while, the child becomes weary and fragmented again, and needs to go back to mother's lap in order to emotionally refuel. There is a rhythm to the child's refueling, the modulation of the distance and separation between the child and the mother, and the ability to forge his way through life on his own. Alcoholics and addicts try to refuel through the use of substances. Instead of using, recovery meetings provide an unconditional source of love and sustenance that is reminiscent of being held in mother's lap.

Another important function that meetings serve is to reduce isolation, which is at the heart of the disease of addiction. The disease of addiction tries to isolate you so that it can have its way with you. Then it locks you in its hold in such a way that you cannot easily get out. I remember wanting to escape from the grips of my addiction, but did not know how. Within the protective wall of the human community, however, it is very difficult for the disease of addiction to survive. The love and power of recovery programs are more powerful than the disease. The disease thrives in isolation, but will die out without it. If you can strengthen the part of you that wants to recover to a large enough degree, it will outweigh the part of you that wants to keep using.

Ambivalence is a normal part of the recovery process. I was ambivalent for several years before I got sober. Part of me wanted to get sober, and part of me wanted to keep using. I wanted both things at the same time, which created enormous internal conflict. I did not know how to release myself from the grips of addiction. The only solution I could think of to resolve the conflict and subdue the difficult feelings was to keep using. After getting into a recovery program, the part of me that wanted health, life, and sobriety was strengthened enough to overcome the part of me that still wanted to use.

My recovery group was the family that I had always wanted. I had been searching for this my entire life; something that would give me a sense of unconditional acceptance, belonging and connectedness. This was the first time ever that I did not feel alone. Feeling a part of my group was the most comfort I had ever felt in my life. I did not have to fend for myself. There was always someone there to lend a hand when I needed it. It was amazing to me how I was always given what I needed, exactly when I needed it.

During the first couple of years in sobriety, I learned how to eat, wake up, go to bed, make friends, cultivate relationships, date, and work as a sober person. Every day was a new learning experience. I was like a baby who had just emerged from the womb; raw, frightened, and insecure. Everything was perplexing to me, and I needed to ask for help with even the most mundane life situations. My recovery sponsor, Karen, was especially helpful in guiding me through early sobriety and the complexities of ordinary life.

I had never had an apartment before. I did not know how to furnish a home or how to clean it. I did not know how to wash my clothes properly. I did not know how to make doctor's appointments and take care of my health. I asked for help constantly, walked through my fears, and slowly learned how to be a person. Slowly but surely, I learned how to live life. I got better and better as the months went on. I asked myself on a regular basis if I was feeling better then the week or the month before, and the answer was always yes.

Working at the Watergate turned out to be an excellent decision, because it was at this job that I first started to acquire self-discipline. I showed up for work on time, in uniform, and did what was required of me. I followed the rules. This was something I had never been able to do before. I learned the basic building blocks of functioning on a daily basis, and gradually developed an internal rhythm. I also learned to how work with others and cultivate interpersonal skills as a sober person. Although I disliked it most of the time, it was exactly what I needed.

Since I had been using on a daily basis since the age of twelve, I had missed out on a lot of important behavioral and psychological development. I was now a twenty-seven year old with the psychological development and real-world experience of a twelve year old. It felt very surreal. All of a sudden, there were five different types of Coca Cola. The last I had remembered, when I was fifteen years younger, there were only two sodas, Coke and Pepsi. How had I missed out on all these changes in the world? It was as though I had been asleep for the past fifteen years, and had missed out on everything that had happened. Now, I was awake and in the real world for the first time in a long time.

It was a profoundly frightening experience. Everything scared me all the time. I saw people around me at meetings who had been sober longer than I; they were calm, happy, and confident. More than anything else, I wanted confidence. I hated my feelings of insecurity, which made me feel that I was inherently less than other people. I hoped that I could attain what I saw in the people around me. I was told that this would be possible if I continued to do the work. What work? The work of recovery was going through difficult feelings without using drugs and alcohol, asking for help, growing, changing, making healthy choices, and dealing with life as it really is.

10

CHOOSING RESPONSIBILITY

Throughout the first couple of years in recovery, I was plagued by the pain of not knowing what to do with my life. I had an excellent education and had been working beneath my potential. I knew it, and did not know what to do about it. My life seemed wrong. Was there anything better in store for me? I could not figure out which direction to take to advance myself.

I knew deep inside that I was meant to do something meaningful, but was at a complete loss to figure out what it was. I waited. Then I waited some more. Then I waited even longer. The answer did not come. I wondered if and how my purpose was ever going to be revealed to me. I wanted to know what I was supposed to do with my life. These were very difficult questions for which I was not prepared. There was no handbook or guide.

I felt stuck. I was sober, but so trapped that I was in despair. I knew that I was supposed to have a purpose and a profession, but I had no idea where to start. I saw others in the world with their careers and with families. I was baffled as to how they got there. They were successful, and felt good about themselves. How did they do it? How do you build a life?

What I did not realize at the time was that building a self and a real life first required acquiring discipline and healthy habits. I already was building my life from the inside out, because I had started working on the insides when I got into recovery. The more slowly that progress in recovery occurs, the more solid a foundation there is to build upon.

Everyone else seemed to know what they were supposed to be doing, and I did not have a clue. Where did everyone else learn all of these skills? I felt as though my life was being wasted as I worked in hotels, sales, and administrative positions. I worked in some of the finest establishments in the country with upper-class clientele, but always in a service capacity. I felt that if I could not live the life I really wanted, at least I could work around the people who were living the life I wanted. Maybe I could learn from them and come to understand something about their lives and how they got there.

I realized that my discomfort could potentially lead me to be self-destructive. I was angry that I could not figure out what to do with my life. The anger started to become toxic for me, because I did not yet know how to channel it to take constructive action on my own behalf. I waited and waited for the answers to come, but they were still not coming. This was an agonizing time, because I was feeling all of these painful feelings without anesthesia.

At the same time, I was in a relationship that also was not working well. I was dating a man, Miles, who lived in Baltimore. We met at a popular downtown restaurant called The Owl Bar. I was commuting back and forth several times during the week to see him. He was extremely volatile, and was prone to fits of rage and demonic possession. I knew that this was not going to be my last relationship, but I was totally enmeshed in the drama. The relationship consumed a lot of my time and energy and prevented me from focusing on doing what I really needed to be doing—learning how to live my own life. I was so consumed by the ups and downs of the relationship that I barely had the energy to recover from it and focus on my job. After a while, I just got tired. I got so tired of it all that I could not do it anymore, and decided to seek professional help to sort things out.

For the first time in my life, I went into therapy. I wanted a therapist who had expertise with addiction and recovery, as well as cross-cultural issues. I did some research, and managed to find someone who fit the bill. I started going to therapy on a weekly basis and opened up honestly for the first time ever about some of my self-destructive behaviors and attitudes.

This process started to create changes in me. I became more and more committed to my own growth and building a life for myself. I was finally just beginning to understand that if I wanted a fulfilling life, I could not continue to operate the same way that I previously had throughout my life. I needed to take off the mask and look under the surface.

At a certain point, my therapist said a few words to me that I will never forget. She said "Anita, you need to be somebody." I remember this as a turning point because I realized that I was not somebody. It was not enough to look good and try to be with the right people. This shattered the false self, inflated ego and sense of entitlement that had driven my life and decisions for so long. I realized just how much work I actually had to do. Best of all, I became willing to do it.

The painful feelings that I had been experiencing gave me the energy source that I needed to start taking action. I started actively working on finding direction in my life. I took an adult education class that helped me to focus in on potential areas of professional interest. I bought self-help books and started reading and doing written exercises that helped me to sort things out, focus on my priorities, and move forward. As I went through this process, I could feel myself making more and more progress in my awareness of who I really was. I was getting closer to finding my path. I was slowly heading in the right direction.

It seemed that once I became actively engaged in the process, instead of sitting around and waiting for the answer to come to me, the universe started to work with me and guide me toward new ideas and opportunities. One thing led to another, and action led to yet more action. I had been catapulted into a new dimension because of the awakening with my therapist. One small sentence had a life-changing impact. This was an example of the fact that when the student is ready, the teacher will appear.

It was around this time that I went to India for the first time in sobriety. I knew that going to India this time would be different than in the past. Previously, I had used drugs and drank as much as possible when I was there, basically trying to avoid the entire experience. As a child, I had gone to India because I was forced to go by my parents. This time, it was my choice. It was the first time that I had gone alone. This trip meant something.

The journey felt divinely inspired. I could feel myself in the natural flow of the universe. I had the opportunity to experience my family for the first time ever with an open heart. When I arrived at the airport, at least twenty of my relatives were there to meet me. In India, it is customary for the whole extended family to receive and see relatives off at the airport. I immediately felt loved, and had the sense that I truly belonged.

On the way to my aunt Rekha's apartment from the airport, I started crying very hard. My soul was deeply moved by the presence of "my" people. I felt a powerful spiritual connection to the place and everyone there. I could sense the ancient remnants of my soul. I spent three weeks with my relatives, and really got to know them for the first time. I got especially close to my paternal grandmother. She was up in age, and we were kindred spirits. I even looked like a young version of her. We stayed up late at night, slept together, and talked in the dark. It was wonderful.

The attachment was so strong that I cried for eight hours on the way back home to the United States. At the time, I could not figure out what was wrong with me, but I now know that I was doing my childhood grief work and healing profoundly. I experienced the integration of my two cultures for the first time ever. As a sober person, I was able to allow both parts of myself to coexist and contribute to the evolution of my selfhood. Best of all, because I was sober, I was able to let the love in.

When I returned home to Washington, life seemed empty and meaningless. There was no family or primal sense of connection. The lonely existence that I felt in this culture was offset only by one thing; my recovery meetings. They provided a deep sense of psychic connection in my everyday life, even without my family of origin. After being spiritually transformed by the trip, I slowly got back into my usual life.

This meant two things: working and dating. I went through a series of three-month relationships that all fizzled out. I was very discouraged about my romantic prospects. I was meeting lots of guys, but nothing ever seemed to work out. I had tried going out with the good-looking guys, but they were too arrogant and stuck on themselves. The last time, I had tried going out with a not-so-good-looking guy, thinking that he would treat me better than a good looking guy would. He disappeared without explanation after two months, never called, and really upset me. I learned that the ugly guys do not necessarily treat you much better than the good looking ones. So much for that strategy.

I decided to take matters into my own hands and place a personal ad. This was before the time of internet dating, so placing an ad was a courageous move. I thought that it would be better to place my own ad than to respond to someone else's. This way, I would be in control. I could pick and choose, and might not face as much possibility of rejection. I also knew that the chances of meeting Mr. Right through an ad were slim.

The most sensible plan seemed to be to try to simply expand my world and meet new friends. I did not really expect to meet a romantic partner or find a boyfriend. Meeting new people was enough to break the monotony of feeling badly as the result of just having been dumped. New friends could lead to other new friends, and that could lead to who knows what.

I got about thirty-three responses to my ad in the first week. This was exciting, and it was enough to get my mind off of the last guy. One of the new people I met was a man named Eddie. Eddie and I met for coffee, and discovered that we had absolutely no romantic chemistry. We did, however, have friendship chemistry. We started talking on the phone as buddies and developed a nice camaraderie.

Eddie had started graduate school that fall. Halfway through the first semester, we were on the phone, and Eddie was in the middle of midterms. He began to read me questions from his midterm exam, and I started answering the questions. As I was giving him my layperson's answers to his high-level graduate school exam questions, he started telling me that my answers were excellent. I was astonished. In that moment, I found the confidence to apply to my own graduate program. I figured that if I could handle his exam, then maybe I could handle my own.

I had enormous fears about returning to graduate school after my two unsuccessful past attempts while drinking and using drugs. I thought that I was not competent to handle the work, and that I was not good enough to be successful in school. It never occurred to me that the problem had never been in my abilities or lack of competency. The problem was that I was addicted to drugs and alcohol. That was what had gotten in my way. All along, I thought I was not good enough to succeed. Addiction is a thief. It slowly takes everything from you that means anything. This was another way that drugs and alcohol had stolen my selfhood, confidence and self-esteem.

It took a lot of pain and misery in sobriety as the result of working in dead-end jobs to muster the courage to go back to school, but the courage finally came to me. Because of what my therapist had said, the work I had done to find my direction, and the experience of passing someone else's exam, I started to believe that maybe I could really do it. Maybe I was good enough. When you keep trying to do the right thing, the universe will conspire to help you.

I applied and was accepted into a master's program at Catholic University to become a psychotherapist. Returning to Catholic University as a sober person was very different from a few years before when I had been there during my addiction. Here I was at the same university, but I was now living in a new reality and enrolled in a completely different program.

From the very first class, I felt that I was doing what was meant for me by the universe. Each class felt like a spiritual experience. I was totally engaged in the process and was hungry to learn. It was meant to be. This was the first time in my life that I made a choice for myself that was really authentic. In the past, my choices had been guided by what I thought I was supposed to do, based on my perception of other peoples' expectations. Life was about seeking other peoples' approval, instead of living my own life.

I felt a profound difference right from the beginning of the program. It was not an effort to do the preparation for my classes; the drive came naturally from within. Unlike my past experiences in school, I never missed a class, took copious notes, participated meaningfully in every seminar, and fulfilled all expectations outside of class. This was especially foreign to me. Not only did I do what was required, but I did not procrastinate. I got most of my papers finished early. I finally discovered the secret to succeeding in school: show up and do the work. What an amazing concept.

The first semester was terrifying. I did not have any confidence in my abilities, but decided simply to try do my best. The anxiety was profound, but the antidote to my anxiety was action. I got straight A's throughout the entire master's program. My drive and motivation never abated. The discipline that I had cultivated in the past few years working in jobs that I hated was now paying off. I had learned how to show up, organize myself, and tackle big projects one piece at a time. I had acquired the basic skills that I needed to succeed. Although I did not realize it at the time, my past experiences had prepared me well for what was to come.

11
SPARKLING

I was now in my early thirties and in graduate school full-time. I was dating a lot, sober, fully-alive, energetic, and eager to experience life to the fullest. I had a friend, Jacqueline, with whom I went out a lot. Jacqueline had been an actress, writer, and producer of television commercials for car dealers. She knew everyone. She was beautiful, charming, creative, savvy, brilliant, and energetic. She brought me out into Washington society as an aspiring grown-up.

She taught me about social relations and introduced me to many events that were a step up from where I had ever been before. I was enchanted with our friendship and with all of the new and exciting experiences. We had a natural synergy that led to countless hours of conversation and having lot of fun together. It was always a stimulating and unpredictable adventure.

Going out to clubs and bars as a sober person was very different from when I had done it in the past during the drinking years. I never felt tempted to drink when I was with other people who were drinking. In fact, I felt a new-found sense of ease and confidence about myself because I was sober and in control of myself. I was able to go out, have fun, stay on top of my game, and remember every single thing the next day. This allowed me to expand my world more and meet new people. I was also able to assess situations with a clarity that only comes from a sober mind.

Life was abundant with cultural events, parties, and black-tie occasions. There was always another date. I had spent a lot of time in short, blip-on-the-screen relationships, but found myself bored or always looking around the corner for something else. What was now different was that I no longer cared if I had a boyfriend. Because I had my own direction and purpose in life, I was content to just enjoy people, without expecting them to fill me up.

Washington was full of tuxedo-clad toxic confirmed bachelors who were out in full force every night of the week. They liked to call themselves "players." This meant that a guy was out for socializing and fun, but did not want a relationship. He might go out with you one night, and then with your best friend the next night. It was like high school, all over again, except the guys were in their fifties.

There was always another event to check out, sometimes two or three in one evening. Initially, it was exciting to meet all the new "regular" people. I had been so insulated in my recovery groups that I had not met any non-recovering people in a long time. The nightlife in D.C. was abundant, but redundant. After a while, it was all the same people at every event. They all talked about nothing. Over and over again.

I was mainly focused on school. I wanted to BE somebody, instead of living in the shadow of someone else or waiting for somebody to come along and take care of me. I decided that I had to give myself what I really wanted in my life, and not make my life contingent upon someone else. I was so in love with school that it came before everything and everyone else. This time, I really took it seriously. I loved it with a passion. For once, something else was more important than men and relationships.

I started dating another magnetic, troubled, and of course, unavailable man—Patrick. I met him on a beautiful May evening after the Gold Cup when I was out with Jacqueline at Café Milano. Café Milano was the hotspot of Georgetown; interesting people always came together there. I remember seeing his bright red hair under the soft lighting of the restaurant and feeling as though he was the only man in the cosmos. He was electrifying. I could not help but be taken in by him.

I said hello to him that evening, but had the distinct feeling that I had known him from before. I could not place him. After a while, we put it together. I had met him a couple of times many years prior through our mutual friend, Renee, when he was a bartender at the Third Edition in Georgetown. I felt a strong connection, but also an immediate sense of danger about him.

Why danger? He seemed to be someone who could really hurt me. I did not know why I felt that way. It was intuitive and powerful. Yet, I was attracted to him like a moth to the flame. I could not stop thinking about him. He was not unlike a drink; dangerous and seductive. And I wanted more. Can people affect you the same way a drink or drug can? You bet.

A couple of months later, I was working in an internship at Georgetown University where I had a very unpleasant supervisor. She demeaned my questions, criticized my clothes, and belittled me at every chance. When I asked her for help, she responded with disdain and contempt. I had no clue as to what was happening or why. All I knew was that I was going home in tears and feeling more inadequate every day that I went there.

To make matters worse, on one particularly difficult day, there was a patient on the ward whom I had known from recovery meetings. The staff was surprised to see that he knew me, because he was a homeless person. It was very awkward and uncomfortable, and I did not quite know how to handle it professionally. I called my longtime buddy, John, who suggested I go that evening to a recovery meeting at St. Albans Church where his friend Ron would be, and talk to Ron about the situation.

After meeting Ron a couple of weeks prior through John, I had been running into Ron on the street quite a bit. There was a one-week period when I ran into him on four different occasions in different locations. Every time I turned around, Ron was passing by. I thought that these were very strange coincidences. As we continued to bump into one another, we had started to say hello. Thus, I was comfortable approaching him.

Ron was a very well-seasoned psychiatrist and psycho-analyst, and had also been in recovery for many years. He was twenty years older and wiser, and had a lot more experience than I did. I went to the recovery meeting that night and approached him. He agreed to talk to me. He invited me to go to dinner at Morton's, a popular steak-house in Georgetown. I joined him along with his friend, Jim. The three of us sat and talked, and then left to go home. Ron drove me to my car, and we said goodbye. As we lived near each other, I was driving behind him in the same direction. He pulled over in front of his house, flagged me down, and asked me to come in, which I did.

We talked some more about the professional dilemmas at my internship; the supervisor, the patient who knew me, and confidentiality issues. When the supervisor sub-ject came up, Ron got a big smile on his face, and said: "She hates you." His warmth and honesty were penetrat-ing. This was the most liberating thing I had ever heard, and I immediately felt relief. I knew he was right, but I had not been able to put it into words myself. I had felt the loathing from her, but did not have the insight or courage to acknowledge it. I had been blaming myself and wonder-ing what I had done wrong.

The reality was that I did not belong in that internship. I again went to the school in tears soon afterwards, and they understood the difficulty of the situation and immedi-ately pulled me out of the internship and placed me in a new position at The National Institutes of Health. It just so happened that The National Institutes of Health was directly across the street from The National Naval Medical Center, where Ron was the Chairman of the Department of Psychiatry.

After our initial evening, Ron started calling. I mean, really calling. He would sometimes call five times in one day. He seemed a little anxious, but I was still interested in spending some more time with him. We had our first din-ner date at Tragara, a restaurant in Bethesda, and then went to tea at the Watergate Hotel, where I had worked many years before. Just for fun, we went upstairs to see one of the luxury suites, and then Ron kissed me.

After we went back to the elegant lounge downstairs, we sat and talked. We basically chatted about trivial matters. Then, out of the blue, Ron asked me to marry him. I did not know quite what to say, so I said, "Now, there's an idea.... ." I was surprised, and I was also not sure if he was serious. He was. The man did not waste any time. I guess some of us are quicker than others at going for what we want.

It was as though a force from the universe swooped in and pushed us together. All of a sudden, Ron was in my life in a big way. There was something very powerful and different about him. He was not like other men I had known. He was the real thing. He knew it, and I knew it. There was no stopping the prevailing force that was greater than both of us. Even though I had been involved with Patrick for five months, I could not fight the relationship that was developing at lightning speed with Ron.

Over the past several months, the relationship with Patrick had not been progressing beyond the dating-longing-waiting stage. Patrick was the unavailable, bad-boy Irish redhead that I had been looking for my entire life. I would see Patrick, have a wonderful date, and feel like this was it. Now we would get closer, I thought. Then I would not hear from him for many days. I constantly felt abandoned, undervalued, and disrespected. The distance between us was carefully measured and maintained by him. There was never contact two days in a row. Usually, there was at least a five-day interval between calls.

I always had the uncomfortable feeling that he was just out of reach. This created longing and yearning, but also enormous frustration. I started to get more and more frustrated over time. When the holidays were approaching, I asked Patrick if he wanted to meet my family at Thanksgiving. He said that he did not want to. When he declined my offer, I wrote him off on the spot. I knew that it would never work. It was time for me to overcome the persistent lure of being hooked to the unavailable man. It was at that moment that I turned the corner.

Although I was crazy about Patrick, I did not want to spend the rest of my days wondering and guessing what he would do next, and waiting for him to call. He had the power, and I did not like that. It was torture. As I had sensed in our meeting at Café Milano, he was dangerous for me. My instincts had been correct. He was alluring, but not mature or available enough to be solid relationship material. The only way to take my power back was to get out.

I also felt that another impediment to having a relationship with Patrick was his age. He was a few years younger than me, and even further behind in relationship skills and experience. I did not have the time or the desire to mentor him through his learning. I did not want a boy; I wanted a man. I also did not want anyone practicing on me. No thank you. I was at a turning point; I was trying to break my old cycle. I had no idea how difficult this transition was going to be for me.

Ron had tickets to the very popular Van Gogh exhibit at the National Gallery of Art, and asked me to go out with him on Thanksgiving eve. I decided to go, and I also decided to get close to him. I wanted to see if we were compatible on different levels. We went to the exhibit, and then spent the night together. That date turned into a long weekend at the luxurious Greenbrier resort. We spent six hours driving each way, and talked about everything under the sun.

I was deeply interested in his knowledge of psychoanalysis, as well as in his vast experience with life and recovery. I knew that if we spent some quality time together, I would know whether I could get serious with him. We really got to know each other, and discovered that we were compatible on many levels: emotionally, psychologically, professionally, physically, and spiritually. We were also both committed to being in recovery. This seemed like a winner to me.

It was as though I had arranged my own marriage, as has been done in India for centuries by family members. In India, two people meet after being prescreened by their families, get a sense of one another, and often decide relatively quickly if they are compatible enough to get married. They marry first, and then learn how to love each other. The commitment is made first, and the love comes later. In the United States, it usually happens in reverse. People fall in love, and then try to learn to commit. So far, that method had not been working well for me.

With my history of running from relationships when the going got tough, the approach of making the commitment first was better. I would not have stayed with anyone any other way. I had to be locked in by something that would prevent me from fleeing. I intuitively knew this about myself, and felt that this was as good a chance as I would ever have at creating a partnership with another human being.

What I did not anticipate, however, was the level of conflict inside myself that would have to be worked through. A big part of me did not want to grow up. A significant portion of my reptile-brain psyche wanted to keep chasing the unavailable man who would never really be there or offer me any stability, but would provide lots of excitement. I was not sure if I was really ready to get off the rollercoaster. I felt a strong pull to move in Ron's direction, but it was very difficult to give Patrick up. He also found it hard to give me up.

When I finally decided for sure to marry Ron, I had to break it off with Patrick. This was no easy task, because now that I did not want him anymore, he had to have me. He fought a very hard battle to try to win me back and get me to leave Ron. I came home regularly to long hand-written love letters, flowers, and gifts. He asked mutual friends to call me to try to persuade me to not get married. They said that I was making the biggest mistake of my life.

I secretly feared that this was true. I also was angry, because I thought that Patrick was only fighting for me because his own ego was hurt. It never really felt like his efforts were about being with me; it seemed like they were more about his not losing. I felt that if I stayed with Patrick, I would not be able trust him to follow through on the things he was promising about how our relationship would be different. I had a sense that he would try to win me back, and then revert back to the way he had always been with me—unavailable. This strengthened my conviction to move in the other direction, although I did so with enormous pain, doubts and confusion.

I knew that the opportunity with Ron would soon pass me by if I did not take it. Even with Ron, it was a gamble, because there was still quite a lot I did not know about him. I was attracted and secured by the fact that he had been sober for over twenty years. I did not want to worry about marrying a drinking alcoholic or someone with other active addictions. My history had been, even in sobriety, to choose men who were psychologically unhealthy or in some other way not good for me. They were fun and interesting, but not appropriate partnership material. I had to make a very difficult decision.

Up until we took our marriage vows, and even afterwards, I was very conflicted. I felt deeply pulled in two directions at the same time. My head told me to be with Ron for all the right reasons; compatibility on many levels and the possibility of a solid partnership. Ron was a mature man who knew who he was. He was a Captain in the United States Navy and a very well-accomplished psychiatrist who had treated members of first families. He was clearly an upstanding solid citizen. He was also the most adorable human being I had ever met. He had it all: he was established, powerful, and respected, in addition to being brilliant, handsome, irresistible and magnetic.

I also knew that at his age, which was fifty-six at the time of our marriage, he was not going to want to keep jumping around. This was favorable, because I did not ever want to go through a divorce. If I got married, I wanted to stay married. After living through my parents' bitter divorce, I never wanted to experience one myself. I had always felt that if I ever married, I would be committed for life, no matter what. For me, divorce was not an option. Ron had been married before, and this was going to be his last go-round, according to him.

Yet I was constantly nagged by longings for Patrick, which were based on my visions of what could have been, rather than what actually was. I was a captive of fantasy. The idea of being with him was almost like a drug-induced state that could only be achieved by wanting something I could not have. Deep inside, I knew that if I stayed with Ron, he would further my evolution. If I stayed with Patrick, I would further his evolution. I knew I had to choose what was going to be better for me in the long run. This was one of the first times in my life that I had really contemplated acting in my own best interest in the realm of relationships.

Ron also went through a lot of his own angst. Having been married before, he was very anxious about the possibility of marring again and divorcing. He had had several failed marriages and three children along the way. His youngest child was eight when we met, and he was still processing the ending of his last marriage. I could see that he was even more conflicted than I was, but he could not stay away. He would call compulsively numerous times in one evening, demonstrating high anxiety, and thereby increasing mine. I was not sure why he was acting erratically. He was driving me nuts. Was he crazy? Was it a good idea for me to even take this risk?

I was discussing the pros and cons of getting married with my friend, Jacqueline. She advised me that at a certain age, it is better to have been married and divorced than to never have been married at all. I could always get a divorce, she said, and it would not be the end of the world. Maybe this was just supposed to be a practice marriage. I really respected Jacqueline's advice. She was slightly older than I, and had a lot more worldly experience. She had been married and divorced, and really understood how things worked. Jacqueline knew how to get out there in the world and really experience life. Her energy and spirit brought enormous vitality to everything she touched. Her presence was always magical.

Her encouragement to simply try was all that I needed to move forward. How would I feel if I did not give it a chance? I was not getting a lot of encouragement anywhere else. My parents were out of the loop and did not quite know what to say. They were lovingly detached and knew me well enough to know that I would make my own decisions regardless of what anyone said. So they stayed neutral and let me work through this one on my own. I realized that my only regrets in life have been things that I did not do, never anything that I did do. I made my decision in that conversation with Jacqueline, and went ahead with the marriage.

Ron planned the wedding in Laguna Beach, California at a gazebo at Heisler Park, overlooking the ocean at sunset. I did not invite my parents or friends from the east coast because I did not know if I was going to have the courage to go through with the wedding. I did not want to bring everyone all the way out to California, change my mind at the last minute, and feel pressured to go through with it just because people were there. I wanted as little pressure as possible. It was terrifying enough with just the two of us.

I had one friend in Los Angeles whom I asked to come to give me away. Frank was a big, tough Italian from Brooklyn who knew how to handle anything. Nothing bad could happen when Frank was around. He was protective, funny and very cool. I knew that I could do anything with him around, and it would be okay. I felt really safe with Frank. After all, we had gotten sober together in Georgetown many years earlier. This was equivalent to coming out of the womb together. There was very little that we had not shared with one another during those early days of learning how to live. Frank had been the first person to make me laugh during those dark days, and our bond was deep. He was the big brother that I never had.

I felt as though I was getting ready for my funeral. I could feel myself about to die at one level. There was no way that I could continue living my old life as a married person. I had no idea what being married was really about, because I had never even seen a real marriage that worked. There was no point of reference. All I had were fantasies of being taken care of and rescued by an all-knowing and all-loving man who would make it all okay. I was soon to find out that I had to give up my fantasy life and learn to live in reality. I could not expect my husband to anticipate and meet my every need. Who was I going to be now? What is marriage supposed to be like?

Ron and I were forty-five minutes late for the ceremony because we got into a huge fight as we were getting ready to leave. We barely made it at all. Both of us were so anxious that we freaked out at the same time. Why? It was hard to say. We were both ambivalent about getting married. Perhaps we were trying to push one another away. Or were we testing to trust? Whatever it was, it was not pretty. I showed up in tears. I could not even explain what the fight was about. I did not know. There was no way to make sense of the hurricane of insanity except to say that we were both terrified and acting out our fear.

We arrived at the setting of the wedding. It was sunset at the ocean on New Year's Eve. I wore a black cocktail dress, and Ron was in a tuxedo. We were married by a new-age California clergyman. The ceremony was short, strained and uncomfortable, but we got the job done. It was as though an invisible power had pushed us through the experience. There was no turning back, and no fighting it. It was meant to be. However, I was such a wreck that I could not enjoy any of it. I was too busy going to pieces.

Ron had asked two of his friends, Don and Sheila, from New port Beach to be at the wedding on his behalf. Don and Sheila were there with bells and whistles. Sheila even gave me something old, new, borrowed, and blue. I had never met her before the ceremony. It was a strange scene. Ron and I barely knew each other, he did not know Frank, and I did not know Don and Sheila. Basically, no one knew anyone at the wedding.

After the ceremony, we all went out for middle-eastern food. Ron and I continued fighting, and I was in tears the entire evening. Don, Sheila, and Frank were at a loss for what to do or say. It was very awkward. By the end of the evening, I was on the phone with my mother, deeply regretting what I had just done. I was sure I had just made the biggest mistake of my life.

This was going to be very difficult situation no matter what I did from this point on. I knew there was no easy solution. If stayed and tried to work it out, I knew I was going to go through hell. If I left, I would go through another kind of anguish, and possibly regret it for the rest of my life. Was I going to be able to give myself a chance to have what I really wanted in my life? Was I willing to do the work? I did not know.

The emotional effort involved in creating a successful relationship was going to be much more gut-wrenching than anything I had ever encountered before. But then again, I had never actually stayed in a relationship long enough to really try to resolve issues and reap the rewards. I had always just run away, or pushed the other person away when things got tough. This had been my pattern for years and years. It had seemed to work, until now. It was time to stop running.

12
MARRIAGE

Most couples get to know each other, and then they marry. In our case, I was the other way around. We got married first, and then got to know each other. It was sort of like an arranged marriage, arranged by ourselves instead of our families. We both assessed the situation, and made a choice based on compatibility on multiple levels. It was the best way for us, because we never would have stuck it out otherwise. One of us would have run if we had not been legally bound together.

Getting married forced me to learn to work things out. In the past, I had used the "cut–and-run" approach to managing conflict, which had gotten me an extended string of three to nine-month relationships. I grew tired of this cycle, and wanted to learn how to have a lasting relationship. I needed to be locked in so that I would hold still and do the work required to form a healthy relationship with another person.

Prior to our marriage, Ron and I had both been on our own for a long time. Ron had not been married for the last ten years. I had lived alone for the last ten years as well, after leaving my father's house in Baltimore. I had never lived with anyone in sobriety before, so cohabitation was a different experience. Ron had been married several times, and was extremely fearful about trying again and failing. I had never even tried marriage before and had little faith that it would work. However, I was going to give it my best shot.

Who was this person? How was this ever going to work? What made a marriage successful? I had no answers to any of these questions. I had to take into account another person's interests, preferences, and choices all the time. Part of the challenge was that I did not really understand Ron very well. I would make assumptions that were incorrect at every turn. I constantly misread him and his intentions. I had no idea how much more I had to learn.

The early days of our marriage were very tumultuous. Ron and I did not really know each other well enough to comprehend or empathize with one another. We were both terrified that we had made a mistake and were both constantly threatening to leave. We knew that it was going to be a lot of work to learn how to live together and love one another. It seemed like an overwhelming task.

On a regular basis, I lost hope about us making it. I became somewhat isolated and depressed. I was overwhelmed by the demands of my new life, and found little time for my former life. My old world was familiar and fun. I had had lots of friends, both male and female. I had lived a spontaneous life, never having to answer to anyone and pretty much just doing as I pleased all the time. Life had been a carefree, unending adventure. I often romanticized my old existence, and doubted my decision to marry.

Life had changed drastically in a very short period of time. Within months, I was married to someone who came from a completely different universe. Ron was from an established, professional world, in which he had many high-level responsibilities. He had worked with VIP's, members of Congress and Senate, and had been involved in major national, international, and professional events in the field of psychiatry, addictions, and recovery. He was a very accomplished and experienced person with many prominent associates. I did not fully comprehend the scope of who he was when I married him. Because I barely knew him, I thought that he was just a really adorable guy that I could not resist.

My new married world was highly structured, with many commitments and pressures. At this time, I was finishing my training as a psychotherapist and simultaneously starting my own practice. Ron and I both had rigorous time demands and busy schedules. Due to our frequent and intense conflict, I constantly thought about leaving, and I'm sure he did too. It felt so hopeless at times that leaving seemed like the only option.

It would have been easy to leave because I owned an unrented furnished condo, and I could just pick up and go back there with little inconvenience. It was not even very far away. I could literally move back to my former home in two minutes. It was very tempting. But I never did. With so much on our plates, the fights really took it out of us. Somehow, we always recovered, and kept trying. There seemed to be a powerful force that kept us together, no matter how difficult things got. At the end of the line, something always happened to restore my faith. It was uncanny.

I did not know how to blend our two worlds. The mechanics of living together were a challenge. I was very neat and orderly when I had lived alone. I controlled everything and kept it in its place. Ron was the complete opposite. The first time I saw his house, I was amazed that he would even bring someone inside the house when it was in such disorder. There were clothes and papers everywhere, and nothing was organized. The room looked as through a cyclone had just come through. Ron did not even seem embarrassed about it. I was mortified. We had completely different standards about what was normal.

We had very different likes and dislikes. Ron preferred darker antiques, and I preferred light colored, modern Italian and Scandinavian furniture. He liked lots of furniture and things in the home, and I preferred it very bare and sparse, with clean surfaces. When I moved in to his house it was fully furnished, but he agreed to make some changes in order to make me feel more comfortable. He had the floors lightened, got rid of some furniture, repainted, and opened up the living and dining room area into one large space. It meant a lot to me that he was willing to try to bring my spirit into his home.

I was working at a substance abuse treatment program in the mornings. It provided me excellent training in the substance abuse field, as well as a professional family. During struggles with Ron, I was often relieved to be able to go to work and be with patients and colleagues. I was fortunate enough to become part of an outstanding organization very early on in my career and remained there throughout my residency and even after I grew my own practice. In the beginning, I internally resisted having to work for someone else in order to obtain independent licensure, but ultimately became grateful to have the opportunity to cultivate and maintain relationships with top notch professionals who are still invaluable teachers and resources to this day.

Ron and his colleagues also mentored me professionally. It was infinitely valuable to have someone with whom I could discuss clinical as well as practice management issues at home, whenever I needed to. This propelled my professional progress forward by leaps and bounds. Ron also taught me a lot about psychoanalysis, a field in which he had earned a PhD after becoming a psychiatrist. This added enormous depth and understanding to my work with patients, as well as in my own personal growth. Whether I wanted psychoanalysis or not, I got plenty of it at home.

I had a misperception about what being a couple actually meant. I thought that it meant that both people were one. This is what I saw in the movies and on television. It was not, however, what I ever saw in real life. I have since come to realize that being in a healthy couple is really about two people who are both whole and complete coming together to share their lives. Another person can never really complete or fix you. You must do it for yourself and maintain yourself emotionally. Above all, it is crucial to hold on to yourself and retain your individual personhood.

One of the biggest mistakes that a woman can make is to lose herself in a man. He is not your God, nor your parent. Do not try to turn him into something he is not. You need to behave as an equal and keep your own life together. It was me who was responsible for the isolation and lack of joy that characterized my early married life.

Because Ron was older, he had a more established life. I mistakenly thought that it would be better for me to try to blend into his life, rather than continue to build my own.

I made the mistake of abandoning myself and my own life when I got married. It was not Ron's fault. He did not try to suppress or isolate me. I did it to myself. It was my decision to stop connecting with myself as well as with my old friends. It was also my choice to not reach out to make new ones. Having separate friends is a vital part of any relationship. It is crucial to keep your own individual support system intact and evolving.

When I met Ron, I had a full, but single person's life. I had few couple friends. Most of my friends were unattached people who were mainly interested in dating and having fun. These friends had been collected over decades and knew me as my single self. When I met Ron and got married so quickly, no one, including me, could process my change of status. It was a shock to most of my friends, who did not know what to make of it. They just stepped back and waited. And I did nothing to integrate them into my new life.

I literally threw my own selfhood away, and believed that I was supposed to become an extension of Ron and embrace his way of living life. I started eating the food he ate. I adopted his views about people, places, and things. I stopped thinking for myself, and found myself even verbalizing his views about issues to others. I began to live his life instead of mine.

This faulty form of self-abandonment caused me to develop feelings of resentment and victimization. He had not victimized me; I had victimized myself. Because I did not realize this, I blamed him. I felt sorry for myself for not having a self. I did not have the support system that Ron had. I had abandoned my support network completely. He had continued to cultivate his own network, and was not about to throw it away just because he got married.

Over time, I began to realize what I had done to myself. After being in enough pain for a long enough time, I started to awaken to the reality that codependency had caused me to lose my own spirit. I needed to be responsible for my own happiness. I gradually started to take steps to rebuild my life. This was a slow, but steady process. It required connecting with myself first, and then reaching out to connect with others.

As my desire to participate in my own life increased, I found that I reached out into life more and more. My energy level increased dramatically. I started going to bed earlier, and waking up earlier. The mornings, which used to be an unpleasant time of the day, became a time of nurturing and productivity. I began to practice a morning routine of self-care on a daily basis. Then I ate a nutritious breakfast and began the workday. It became easier to take care of myself and act on my own behalf. I started to feel energized most of the time. I got excited about life again.

I started seeking out friends, and getting together with them regularly. I contacted everyone I could from my past and my childhood and resurrected old relationships. Reconnecting with old friends got me in touch with parts of myself that had been lost and buried over the past several years. I started attending more recovery meetings, and expanding my areas of personal growth. This led to yet more people in my life, and more opportunities to be of service to others. Most importantly, I started focusing more on what I could give, and less on what I could get.

I began to develop new interests that did not involve Ron. I started a peer supervision group for other medical professionals who are also in recovery. I began writing, and accessing my own innate creative energy. I discovered that I could not get the old me back, because I was no longer the same person. But I could get the new me.

All of this had a significant impact on my relationship with Ron. The busier I got, the more Ron was attracted to me. He became more attentive, caring, and thoughtful than ever. He stopped taking me for granted and valued me more and more, because I valued myself more than ever. Instead of my looking to him for my happiness, I was now giving it to myself. Another person really cannot make you happy. You must do it yourself.

Interestingly enough, the more I focused on being responsible for my own happiness, the more I also appreciated Ron. Instead of noticing his shortcomings and deficiencies, I saw more clearly how much he had contributed to my having a beautiful life. He was truly a wonderful man.

I started to feel his love in ways that I had not felt before. I could appreciate all the small things he does on a daily basis that demonstrate his love for me. He has his own way of loving me, and my challenge is to recognize it, and allow it into my heart and life. It is so easy to get caught up in one's model of how it is supposed to be, that it is easy to miss the good that is actually there. The key to happiness is to focus on what you have, rather than getting what you want.

Ron cuddles with me every morning. He calls often and keeps in close touch. He does not make any major decisions without consulting me. He talks to me when he is struggling with something, and trusts my advice. He is good to my family, and goes out of his way to show his love for them. He appreciates my cultivating relationships with his family. He tries to include me in everything in his life. He is always there when I need him. He allows me the freedom to live my life as I choose, and does not try to control my choices. Most of all, I feel like I am the most important person in his life.

The most important relationship principle that I have learned is that a relationship works best when each person is focused on what he can give, rather than on what he can get. The more that I try to give Ron what I want, the more he tries to return the same thing to me. The more that I try to make sure that he is happy and that his needs are met, the more he tries to make sure that I have what I want and that my needs are met. We mirror each other in relationships. Whatever it is that I am putting out is what I am going to get back.

The new me is a vast improvement over the old me. I now have a much more solid sense of self than I ever did. Because of marriage, I have developed a greater breadth and depth of character than I had ever known. They say that if you are good in this life, you will come back as something better in the next life. This has been true in my case.

13

REVOLUTION

In the first couple of years of the marriage, Ron and I both had major issues with anger. Ron had temper tantrums regularly and lost control of his emotions. It could happen at any given time. I never saw it coming. I felt like I was walking on eggshells, and never knew what would set him off. Still worse, I never knew how I would react, or whether I could contain my own anger. I lost it too. I was a passive-aggressive reactor and screamer. Once I got really angry, it was hard to turn it off.

Ron would lose control of his anger in a different way. Whatever was in his path during an outburst was vulnerable to destruction. He would trash his own things, or mine, depending on where we were in the house. When he would break things, I would get terrified, and sink into even deeper retaliation and despair. Ron had struggled with his temper for decades, and feared that at his age he could not change.

From day to day, there was no predicting whether we would be fighting or sane. Several times a week we got into major conflicts, and it was extremely difficult to even remember what had happened. All of a sudden, we would be in the middle of a storm that escalated into insanity. It was like an emotional tornado that came out of nowhere, sucked us up, swept us off, and devastated everything in its path. The conflicts could start over the smallest little thing. They would usually end simply because we both got too tired to keep fighting. Sometimes it was just easier to stop struggling and try to go back to our everyday lives.

Because of my parents' divorce, I was very dedicated to my marriage. I absolutely did not want a divorce under any circumstances. That would have been my worst nightmare and biggest perceived failure. Driven by my own pride, I was determined and devoted to making the marriage work. I had waited thirty-six years to marry and felt committed to my choice. I wanted to overcome the issues at hand no matter what it took.

Ron had tried repeatedly to marry, but had not been able to make it work in the past. When he met me, he was terrified to even try again for fear of failure, but was unable to stop himself from marrying me. When we fought, his solution to every problem was to get divorced. This time however, he had married the wrong girl, because I was not so quick to give up. My persistence and willingness to stick it out kept us in the game.

When two therapists are married to each other, the conflicts can cut deeply when one person starts to analyze the other's behavior. Ron and I knew exactly how to push each others' buttons, and did so even more effectively armed with clinical training. Thus, the commonality of our professions could work for or against us, depending upon how we used our energy.

Every time that Ron brought up divorce, I told him that he could leave if he wanted to, but that I was going to stay and try to work it out. Despite himself, he always eventually came around. He kept trying to work things out. I recognized this, and gave him credit for doing what he could. I also think he did not want me to progress beyond him. The more I worked on things, the more progress I made in my relationship skills. When I learned to behave better than he did, he wanted to catch up to me. If he gave up, I won. Competition can sometimes work positively for your relationship.

In the early years of the marriage, Ron was the recipient of the stored-up reservoir of anger with my parents. The anger with my mother was because of my perception that she had not been there for me emotionally due to her own difficulties when my father left us. I felt that I had to be her parent, and that no one was there for me. My father was gone, and she was trapped in her own pain. Thus, the focus was on taking care of her, and I felt unattended to.

The anger with my father was for leaving me. I did not believe that he really loved me if he was capable of leaving. Underneath, it was really hurt, not anger that I felt. I had been abandoned at the age of six, and had spent my entire life trying to cover up the pain of the loss of my father. Even though I medicated my loneliness with drugs, alcohol, and people for so long, the feelings never really went away. They re-emerged in full force after I got married.

All of the hurt, anger and rage came out at Ron, and I never even saw it coming. When we had conflicts, I would lose control of my emotions. Once I got angry, I could not stop. It was like getting drunk, except on anger. It was a binge without alcohol, complete with a nasty long-lasting emotional hangover the next day.

In the early years, it would take days, sometimes even weeks, to emerge from the anger and get back to normal after a fight. Of course, I blamed him for all of this, saying that he had provoked me. If he had been a better person, I would not have been feeling all of this anger. I did not realize that he was not responsible for my feelings. I was. I had to own my own part in what was happening and take responsibility for working on it.

I went back into individual psychotherapy, and this time it was with a therapist named Paul. In our first session, we talked about why I was there.

"I'm very angry with my husband. He treats me badly, and we can't get along."

"How long have you been married?" Paul asked.

"A few months."

"What do you want?"

"I don't know," I said. "My husband and I are having a really hard time. I think that maybe I should leave."

"That's okay with me; what do you want me to do about it?" he said.

"I don't know," I said. I was stunned. He did not try to talk me out of it. This was no big deal to him. He did not try to fix it. He was so matter-of-fact that it took the wind out of my sails. He simply gave me permission to leave. Once I internalized the reality that I really could leave, I was not so sure that I wanted to. What was I going to do?

Go back to the apartment that I had just left and pick up my old life again? That did not make sense. I was on the verge of giving up too soon. I left the first session deciding to stick it out a little while longer to see if we could make it work.

I was learning to be a professional person, and also simultaneously to be a wife. It was difficult to handle both of these leaning experiences at the same time. Some days were better than others. I desperately needed help and support, so I stayed in therapy. I went to therapy sessions every week, recounting the difficulties since the previous session. I was always wondering if I should leave the marriage. In every single appointment, Paul would help me to see that I really did not want to leave at that particular time, although I might want to leave in the future. I would leave the sessions feeling like I should give the relationship just a little while longer. This went on for a couple of years.

This is reminiscent of how many people stay sober by just not drinking one day at a time. They may want to drink, but do not drink just for today. Be delaying the present urges to act out self-destructive behaviors for ever-extending periods of time, a person can stay sober indefinitely. This technique also worked to keep me in my marriage. Just like drinking, I might leave tomorrow, but I will not leave today. Just for today.

I was now also seeing how my personality had been impacted by diminished social support and a lessening of recovery group activities. I became depressed, reactive, dependant, angry, and wanted something outside of myself to fix things. This was who I was before I ever picked up my first drink. I had also regressed emotionally into not taking responsibility for my own choices and feelings. I tried to hold Ron responsible for how I felt.

This approach was really not working well. I kept on wanting him to change in order for me to be happy. If only he would do such and such or stop this or that behavior, life would be grand. I really saw him as the problem. I lost sight of the fact that I was responsible for my own happiness and what was happening in my life. I had also forgotten that it is not so much what happens, as my reaction to it that determines the quality of my experiences.

Throughout the first couple of years, things slowly started to improve. We both hung in there and kept trying. We both stayed in therapy and went to more recovery meetings. I had slacked off on going to meetings during the years I was in school and in the early part of the marriage. I had gotten so busy that I was not prioritizing my own self-care and recovery.

The fights gradually grew further apart and less intense. Things were actually improving. I remember the first time that I saw Ron laugh. I had never seen him laugh about anything for the first two years. I did not know he could. When I tease him about this now, he says that nothing had been funny. I finally started to see him lighten up and joke, and he started to make me laugh too. He actually had a wonderful sense of humor and was very witty. He was also brilliant and learned, and was fascinating to talk to. I was finally just getting to really know him.

The reality was that with time and hard work, Ron and I both grew. We both learned to control our anger by responding, rather than reacting to it. I learned that anger as an emotion is not a bad thing. It is a signal that something needs to be addressed or changed. It is also a powerful energy that needs to be managed and channeled properly. Yes, I did need to address the issues that were truly important, but there were other things that I needed to simply let go.

It is important to discern the things that can be changed from those that cannot. Mostly, the things that could be changed fell into one category: anything to do with me. The things that could not be changed generally fell into another category: anything to do with him. Over time, I have also learned what matters and what does not. If you want to, you can make an issue out of almost anything. Some things are really just not that important.

I also learned that I could use my anger in very constructive ways for myself. Whenever I feel really angry now, I try to ask myself what I can do for myself, not what I can do against the other person. This has brought me closer to my own spirit, and continues to take me to higher levels in my life. Early in the marriage, when things were very difficult, I got my doctorate in psychology because I was angry, and did not know what else to do with the energy. I channeled my power into something positive for myself. I accomplished something beyond my expectations simply because I gave it a try and used anger as the energy source to forge ahead. This was a giant leap forward from my past self-destructive coping mechanisms.

Later, I was chronically angry that we could not work out our housing situation. When we got married, Ron and I lived in his home. His will called for the house where we lived, which he bought before we met and is his primary asset, to be left to his three children and myself in the event of his death. Thus, it would be split up four ways. So, if Ron passed way, I would not only have to grieve the loss of my husband, but I would also have to promptly look for a new place to live.

This seemed like too much to have to do all at once, and I agonized about the situation for several years. Ron and I were at an impasse. It did not seem fair, but we both understood one another's situation. His home was the only major asset he had to leave to his children. Naturally, he wanted to give them a fair share of what he had. For me this was very problematic because I did not own my own home and I wanted to be able to maintain stability in my own life. After much conflict about this dilemma, I was guided towards a solution.

I finally took charge of this by focusing on my self-care. What could I do for myself to resolve this? I had an unexpected break in my schedule on a Monday, called a real estate agent, and looked at five properties that afternoon. When I saw what would be my own future home, I immediately fell in love with it. I intuitively knew that this was the place for me. The very next day, I made an offer, and by Wednesday, I had a contract. Using my own income and resources, I bought a gorgeous, newly renovated apartment for myself close to his house in Georgetown. I was able to secure my future needs.

This was one of the most empowering things I had ever done for myself. I did not even consult Ron about my decision. I knew it was right. I also knew it would solve a lot of the issues that had been plaguing us for some time. Ron was very supportive of my decision, and was also relieved that I had come up with a creative solution to our dilemma. I spent quite a bit of time and energy furnishing the home to my taste, and have created a place that truly reflects my own spirit.

Moving in to someone else's home can be psychologically challenging at many levels. Ron and I did not have the same preferences. We were not even from the same era. Prior to having my own home, I always felt like a visitor in someone else's space. It never really felt like mine. Instead of trying to change each other, we accepted our differences and each gave ourselves what we really wanted.

Sometimes couples have unconscious expectations of one another to provide what they never got as a child. When Ron and I were first married, I wanted him to be the father that I always wanted who would never abandon me. He was a Captain in the United States Navy, and was required to travel several times every year. Ron was sensitive to my vulnerabilities and attempted to reassure me in the ways that he could. Prior to each trip, he made sure that I had groceries, medicine, and anything else I might need. He always called me every day while traveling, so that we could maintain our sense of connection. Most importantly, he returned home from every trip and never abandoned me.

Ron wanted me to be the mother that he never had who would stay steady and not abandon him. Although I regularly contemplated leaving, I never did. I learned to not run, work on myself, and stay put. This healed Ron's childhood wounds that resulted from being abandoned by his mother when he was regularly sent to stay with his grandparents and was consequently separated from his family.

In trying to repair our ancient childhood wounds, and were testing each other to see if we could trust one another. My anger tested Ron's willingness to stay with me and work through our conflicts. Ron's temper tantrums were part of his testing me to see if I would stay with him. I often felt controlled, as I had felt growing up with my mother. It is not uncommon to re-experience childhood feelings in a marriage, particularly in the early years. These early conflicts reappear and then can be worked through in order to get to the healing. Then the marriage can survive and thrive. Thus, our unconscious unresolved childhood needs around abandonment were being acted out and repaired in our dramas. With time, things slowly got better. With both of us working on our own issues separately, we continued to make progress.

I believe that you always match up with someone with whom you can complete your unfinished psychological work. Ron and I have both managed to heal our deepest childhood wounds as a result of working on our own issues and staying together. Perhaps our marriage is not even just for us. Our relationship has been a force multiplier. We have both been able to do much more good for others because we are together than we would have been able to do if we were apart. Sometimes the universe works in uncanny ways.

14

THE OLDER MAN

If the French rule for marriage is for the man to be twice the age of the woman plus seven, Ron and I got it pretty close to perfect. He was fifty-six and I was thirty-six. For me, it was just right. I had always loved older men. They always seemed much more interesting. They seemed like real men. They were also well-mannered, and more thoughtful than younger men. I feel that there are many advantages to marring an older man, as well as many challenges.

The differences between a younger woman and an older man can be vast, but can be exceptionally complementary. A younger woman can bring vitality and energy to an older man's world. An older man can bring depth and richness to a younger woman's life, with a wealth of experience that only a longer life can bring. Having someone who was settled and established allowed me to evolve and develop my own life from a base of stability. As an older man, Ron had much more to offer in terms of experience, wisdom, and knowledge of how the world works. He knew how to get things done. His experience and knowhow saved me inordinate amounts of time and energy. This allowed me to grow and progress much faster than I would have without him.

One challenge that occurs with an older man is that he has a longer past than you do. That means that he probably has a former spouse or two, and they may still be in his life. This is not at all a threat to the relationship. It is very important to be friendly and accepting of the former women in his life. They are probably having a harder time accepting you than you are of them. Remember that it did not work out with them. He is with you now because he wanted something better.

When Ron and I first married, I felt very threatened by his last wife, Ruth. I knew that he was not over her. Plus, they had had a child together, Tara. Ron and I had not had a child. I felt that Ron and Ruth were the "real" family because they had procreated. This activated my ancient feelings of being different than other people, of not feeling good enough, and of feeling like an outsider. I thought that Ron and I could not be a "real" family without also having a child. I resented his ex-wife, Ruth, because she had something I did not have.

As time went on, I learned that their child was our child too. Ruth was not a threat in any way. This became clearer when she married her own new husband, Eric. She was always very kind, gracious, and respectful towards me. She even sent us flowers for our Indian wedding ceremony on our five-year anniversary. Now we all even get together for a meal every now and then. We have become a family. We all accept, respect, and care for each other. I think this has been most beneficial for Tara, who does not have to see her family as completely split off. She has points of reference in which there has been integration among both of her families.

When it comes to his family, I have found that the best approach is to treat his family exactly as yours. If you have married him, then his family is now yours and your family is now his. My life has been greatly enriched by my husband's family. Ron has two brothers, one sister, and three children. His two sons also have their own children, which results in a large extended family. It has been wonderful to be friends with his two older children. Tara, the youngest, was eight years old when we married. I have had the opportunity to be both a stepmother and a friend to her at the same time. We have had a wonderful relationship throughout the entire marriage.

I think it is best to try not to be too parental as a stepparent. If there are stepchildren who dislike you, I would recommend taking the high road, and trying not to react in kind. Children from divorced families sometimes have an underlying wish that their parents will reunite, and any new partner is seen as less desirable than the biological parent. In this case, it is best to back off, but also to continue to be as loving as possible towards them. In general, being thoughtful of his family and involving yourself with them will lead to greater unity and an increased sense of intimacy in the marriage.

Due to our age difference, Ron's friends were all much older than I was. This was not a problem in the sense that I had always had a lot of older friends. However, I had also always had younger friends too. Given the fact that I was not interacting with many my own friends, I was left with only his friends, who were basically unfamiliar to me. Over time, I redeveloped my own network of friends, plus I had his friends. This expanded and enriched my world greatly.

An older man may be concerned about holding on to you, and possibly insecure about whether or not you will still be there when he gets even older. He knows that you have more time ahead of you than he does, and that you could find another man if you choose to. You need to give him reassurance when he needs it. I have often told my husband: "I looked for you for thirty-six years. I finally found you, and I know you're the best man for me." With humor, I then added, "I'll tell you what, I'll wait another thirty-six years, and if somebody better comes along, I'll take him." Ron loved that response so much that he has used it with his patients in his psychiatry practice.

An older husband may experience sexual dysfunction problems. If this is the case, do not be dismayed. It is not your fault. It is very common among older men, but the marvels of modern medicine have made it possible for older men to enjoy much longer and active sex lives than in the past. Do not hesitate to pursue medical or therapeutic help for these issues. Be proactive and creative in your sexual life together.

His experience and knowledge will be helpful in the bedroom too. You probably will not have to teach him as much as a younger man. If you have chemistry, you will find a way to feel sexual intimacy and closeness. Keep an open mind, relax, and be yourself. This is not his first rodeo.

The more relaxed you are, the better it will be for both of you. He may have sexual performance anxiety. It is very important that you put him at ease, and not add to it. I often had to say to Ron, "Don't worry at all; it's going to be great." And guess what—it always was. I had to take the lead in the reassurance. Although it sometimes bothered me, it was always worth it.

Property issues are often a source of conflict in marriage, but can be even more so in a marriage with an older man. If both parties have equivalent assets, they can be joined or kept separate and distinct, depending on the situation at hand. It is crucial to secure your basic needs so that your life can go on should your older spouse predecease you. Property and wills need to be discussed openly so that there are no surprises later. Ron is the most brilliant man I have ever known. However, he does not always manage his money well. He loves fast horses, Mercedes, and Paris.

Just because someone is older does not mean that they cannot still grow and change. There is no limit to our growth if we are willing to do the work to get there. An older man can be more motivated for change and serenity than a younger man, because he has less time to waste. He wants the remainder of his life to be filled with quality time. Ron and I both took additional steps to get help in dealing with our anger. We both got into enough emotional pain that we were willing to go to more recovery meetings and also to individual psychotherapy. Therapy was especially helpful, because it was a place where I could just focus on me.

Another reality of being married to an older man is dealing with the fear of the loss of one another. I think about this nearly every day. After all the hard work that we have both put into our marriage, we wish it could last forever. However, the fact is that Ron is twenty years my senior and it is possible that I will outlive him and spend some of my years without him. Of course, one never really knows how things will unfold; I could predecease him. But the odds are that I will not. Thus, we both appreciate the fact that each day is a gift.

One of the most romantic things Ron has ever said to me was just before going to sleep one evening:

Ron said, "I don't want to go to sleep."

I asked, "Why?"

He said, "Because when I go to sleep, I'll have one less day with you." This touched my heart deeply because I knew it was true for both of us. Reality can make you really focus on appreciating what you've got, while you've got it, and making the most of each day.

15

FROM SEX TO INTIMACY

I remember the first time a boy ever told me I was sexy. I was nine years old. It happened on the playground at Friends School in Baltimore. The boy was David, an older boy who was a couple of years ahead of me in school. I did not know what it meant, but I knew it was good. I could tell by his tone and the look on his face that being sexy meant having power.

By the time I was eleven, I had started developing as a young woman. I was one of the first in my class to do so. It made me feel older. I also started to think about older boys, because the boys my age were still babies. They grew up much later than the girls, who had a head start. The boys in my class seemed light years behind in their development. The older boys had more experience, knowhow, and sex appeal. They were more interesting.

I thought about boys a lot. All the time, actually. I was obsessed with boys in my school, as well as with teen idols, like Mick Jagger and David Cassidy. The sun rose and set around the male that I was focused on at the moment. Even before I started using drugs and alcohol, I was addicted to boys. They were all that mattered. I thought that the right boy would make my life complete, and then everything would be wonderful.

When I started using drugs and alcohol daily at the age of twelve, this obsession quickly evolved to older guys who also liked to party. It was an adventure to share the experience of getting high and being romantic with someone. It was an intimate experience, even without any physical contact. I sought a deep connection that I thought could only be attained through the medium of a drug.

When I first discovered sex as a teenager, it was inextricably intertwined with drinking and using. It was a powerful drug in and of itself. Once I discovered that I could get a high from my own body, I could not get enough of it. Just like everything else that got me high, sex was a compulsion and something that I thought about and wanted all the time. What was marvelous was that I did not even need another person to get the high. I could do it all by myself. But it was always better with someone else.

Since I looked older than my years, I attracted a lot of older boys. It was the 1970's, and the end of the era of free love. AIDS had not yet come on the scene, so everyone was having a lot of sex, and not worrying about consequences. It was not uncommon to just hook up with people you did not know, and then go about your business. My business was hedonism and enjoying myself as much as possible every day. Sex and drugs were as intertwined as scotch and soda.

During the fifteen years that I was drinking and using drugs, there was little psychological and emotional development that occurred, especially in my capacity for emotional intimacy. My early relationships were all about going out drinking, getting high, having sex, and feeling good. Period. There was no real closeness or working through of issues. When conflicts came up, I either ran away or pushed the other person away. Over and over again. I thought that sex was intimacy. Thus, I never learned much of anything about what it means to have a real relationship until I was much older.

There were lots of men. And a few women too. I cannot even begin to remember them all. What I do remember is that each one was a new exploration. I never let having a boyfriend stop me from having adventures. One of the advantages of drinking and drugging is that you do not have a conscience. You are so cut off from yourself and your value system that it is possible to behave in ways that are discordant with your true self. Lying, cheating, and living a double life are all okay. Any and everything is acceptable in the name of self-gratification and the pursuit of pleasure.

After getting sober things changed, but gradually. Even in early sobriety, my relationships were still toxic and shallow. This pattern persisted for a couple of years. I went through a series of short relationships, but I could not sustain a long-term bond. I was sober, but operating the same way I always had. It was about what I could get rather than what I could give. I was still as self-seeking and wild as I had always been as a drinking person. In the sober light of day, this was not quite as acceptable to me.

Now that I was in my thirties, it was no longer tolerable to just have sex for the sake of it and keep moving on to the next guy. I developed a conscience and values. I began to want a real and intimate relationship with a man. I started to realize that there were more than enough younger women out there to fill my old shoes. In fact, they were replacing me without my consent. The guys my age and even older were looking for girls in their twenties, not grown women in their thirties. It was time for me to grow up.

Fortunately, in sobriety I was able to assess my own behavior with clarity, and learn from each experience. Emotional intimacy started to matter to me. Every time a relationship did not work out, I began to ask myself why. What was my part in it? What about me? I realized that I was the common denominator in all the relationships. It could not possibly have been everyone else's fault all these years. Oh no, what if the problem was not really them after all?

It was no longer simple. I did not have a clue as to where to begin my own inventory. I knew how to blame and find fault in others, but had no experience in examining myself. I used the recovery tools that I knew, but came up short in really getting to the bottom of the exact nature of my shortcomings in relationships. Therapy was extremely helpful in this process.

In the back of my mind, I had previously believed that if I met the right guy, life would just magically work itself out. I had no idea that I needed to do an enormous amount of work on myself before I was going to be relation-ship material. I was looking for someone to save me, but did not realize it. It turned out that the only person who could save me was me.

While sex itself was still wonderful, I now had to deal with the relationship part that went along with it. I could no longer keep sex separate from relationships. At times in the past, I had wondered if I was really a guy deep down inside, because I behaved like the stereotypical male. I constantly sought sex without intimacy. Through therapy, I learned that I was afraid of being vulnerable and of doing the work of learning how to have genuine emotional intimacy.

In sobriety, failed relationships became my teachers, not my tormentors. I learned that I could no longer have sex or relationships without choosing to learn my lessons. The most shocking thing of all was the realization that sex without a relationship was not so much fun. It was really kind of empty. My old high was not working anymore. Now that there was nothing left to anesthetize my feelings, I was going to have to learn how to live a real life and manage my emotions. As a sober person, the feelings were all there: joy, pain, sadness, anger, guilt, shame, lust, and fear, just to name a few. Tolerating the feelings without numbing them or acting out was very difficult, probably one of the toughest parts of being sober.

In ending my relationship with Patrick just before getting married, I resolved the eternal longing for the unavailable man. I had spent my life yearning for that which I could not have, and never wanting what I could have. This had tormented me throughout my entire life and had been a recurrent intimacy-breaker. I could never get very far with anyone. Even after overcoming my misguided sexual focus, I still did not understand anything about the real-world relationship between sex, intimacy, and mature love.

Before meeting Ron, I had a profound internal shift. I stopped waiting for the right guy to come along and fix my life. I decided to do it myself. I bought a small apartment, and also decided to go back to school and develop a career that had meaning for me. Taking responsibility for my own life set me on a whole new path, which ultimately led to being able to have a mature, adult relationship. I had to stop acting like a little girl, and start behaving like a woman who was responsible for her own life. In so doing, I believe that I attracted a very different type of person into my life.

My relationship with my husband was very different from any other right from the start. I chose to be with Ron because I wanted to, not because I needed to. I was not looking for him to save me, because I had already made the decision to save myself. I learned how be vulnerable without running away. I also learned how to communicate my wants and needs without being critical, and to listen and respond to Ron's needs as best I could. He always responded to my needs when I was soft and vulnerable, which made me let go of my old hard-hitting approach. Most importantly, I learned to never stop trying.

Like me, Ron has an extensive past with many relationships. I do not care about his former marriages or affairs. He is with me now, and I know that he is fully with me. We are both secure enough within ourselves to give each other the respect we both deserve. I do not really care what he did in the past, or with whom he did it. In fact, I would rather not know. How would it help our relationship? I deal with him in the here and now, with who he is today. He treats me the same way.

Ron and I both need a lot of personal space. I grew up as an only child, and always had time alone. Ron grew up alone at his grandparents' home in Tennessee and was separated much of the time from his family. After having lived alone for so much of our early and adult lives, we both had been used to having alone time and room to breathe.

The paradox is that loneliness has plagued me my entire life, but solitude has also been restorative and nurturing. In a healthy relationship with yourself, you do not necessarily feel lonely just because you are alone. You are comfortable within yourself, and enjoy your own company. In a healthy marriage, you can be alone or be together, but you are able to maintain your sense of connection with the other person. When you have a secure bond, it is not threatening to the intimacy to have time alone. It nurtures the relationship.

We both decided to trust and love one another. I have found that people generally behave the way that you expect them to. If I expect Ron to treat me well, and treat him accordingly, he does. It also seems that people will generally treat you the way you treat them. If I am loving and thoughtful towards Ron, it is reflected back to me by him. If I am selfish and mean, that is returned to me too. Thus, whatever the other person is doing serves as a reflection. Ultimately, I always need to go back to looking at myself and my own behavior.

Just like taking a drink, acting out with another man might feel good in the beginning, but it would not really fulfill me. I know myself. It would take me down the wrong road. I love my new path too much to give it up. Sobriety gives me the freedom to make my choices based on what makes me feel good about myself, not based on what makes me feel good for a moment.

I am very grateful for all the experiences I had as a young person. They have enriched me tremendously. Most of all, I know that I am not missing out on anything. Therefore, when I finally made the decision to commit fully to someone, I meant it. I never thought that I had what it took to have emotional intimacy, but I did. For nine years, Ron and I have been committed, loyal, and faithful to one another. We have had a wonderful sex life throughout our entire marriage, despite (and probably because of) our age difference. Being willing to sit through the pain, not act out, and try to grow and do the right thing have paid off. I have learned how to have sex and emotional intimacy at the same time. My relationship is as good as they get.

16

CHILDLESSNESS AND FULFILLMENT

As I got into my early 40's, I started to think about whether or not to have a baby. I noticed mothers every-where around me, bonded with their babies and their fam-ilies in a way that I envied. I went to family gatherings and felt like I was the only childless person. I would see fami-lies with children enjoying themselves in the park across the street every Sunday.

Sunday was like national baby day, and I felt like I had missed the boat. Did I forget to do the most important thing in life? Was this something I even wanted to do? I had never really wanted to have a baby, but I had a grow-ing awareness of the passage of time. The reality was that the option was soon going to be taken away by age.

I was at my husband's family reunion in the hills of Ten-nessee in April, 2004. It was a beautiful spring day of fam-ily-fest. Families layered upon one another, all with multitudes of children who were laughing, running, play-ing, and bringing joy to everyone around. The house had belonged to Ron's grandparents and reeked of rich history. There was an outhouse in the yard, on a sizable tract of farmland. It was a picturesque snapshot into southern country life of the 1940's. I had the sensation that not very much had changed there since Ron's grandparents were alive.

I marveled at the cohesiveness of the large group, encompassing all of the smaller family entities. I was reminded of my childhood visits to India at my grandpar-ents' house, where the extended family all lived together. I would wake up out of a dreamy sleep and there would always be a loving lap to hold me. I felt eternally comforted and connected to something beyond myself. At that time, my sense of separateness and aloneness went away.

My father's three brothers, three sisters, and their chil-dren all lived in a joint family structure with his parents in one large apartment in Bombay. The environment was fun, lively, festive, and inviting. There was a lot of laughter, conversation, care, concern for one another, and unconditional acceptance. It was the prescription for loneliness that I had needed my entire life. When I was there, I felt that nothing bad could happen to me and that everything would be okay. I wanted to create that feeling in my own life. Perhaps having a child would accomplish this.

It slowly came to my awareness that now was the time for me to confront my question of whether or not to try to have a baby. I talked about it with Ron and he was open to the idea. He was not overly eager to have a baby, but he was supportive of whatever I wanted to do. He was twenty years older and had already had three children. He would have been content to leave it at that, but he did not want me to feel deprived of the opportunity to have my own children.

I had been on birth control for over twenty-five years, and had never gone off of it for even a day. My ultimate horror had always been the possibility of getting pregnant. I had grown up thinking that having a child would be the supreme state of imprisonment. This was based on what I saw in my mother's life. After all, she had had to deal with me, which was no picnic.

I came to a turning point when I knew that it was now or never. How would I feel at the end of my life if I had never even given myself the chance to confront this issue or find out for sure what I really wanted? I have learned that it has not been the things I have done in life that have caused me regret; it has been the things that I have not done that I have regretted the most, for example, missed opportunities or not having had the courage to act on what I really wanted.

I decided to take myself off of birth control for the first time ever since I was sixteen years old. It felt very purifying, courageous and freeing at the time. I was going to let God decide my fate. If I got pregnant, then I was supposed to have a child. If not, then that would be okay too because it was not meant to be. I knew that the right thing would happen. I was not going to pursue aggressive measures to make sure I got pregnant. I had seen several of my friends go through this unnatural and agonizing process, and it did not appeal to me. I did not subscribe to the urgency to procreate that I saw in so many other women who were my age.

I went through the next several months feeling at peace with my decision. Ron and I discussed how it would all work, and it seemed like a stretch, but possible. I could take time off from my practice, and then hire a nanny when I went back to work. This would not be easy, but I knew that in the end Ron would come through and be supportive. He always had.

In August of 2004, about four months after I had gone off the birth control, I started to not feel well. One Saturday morning I was jogging outside on the streets of Georgetown, and became very dizzy and frightened. I could not walk properly. I felt very weak and off-balance. I had to hold on to the side of a building in order to keep from falling down. I had a very bad spell, but managed to get home.

A few days later, the same thing happened. This time, however, I was not even moving at all. I was sitting in a room full of people, and all of a sudden I felt like I was going to die. I could not even sit there. I was very dizzy, could not breathe, and could not walk. My friend Tommy helped me get to my car, and I went home and tried to get ready for work. This day began a three-week period of nonstop heart palpitations. My heart was palpitating day and night. I could barely hear anything else. I would go to sleep with severe palpitations, and wake up with them all over again. I kept hoping that I would wake up one morning and they would be gone, but they just went on and on and on.

During this time, I slowly became virtually disabled. I was so dizzy every day that I could barely stand up in the shower. I would drive to work with my head leaned back against the headrest in the car for stability. I could barely walk from the car to the building where my office was located in Bethesda. I was extremely dizzy, and even normal sunlight was so overpowering that I constantly felt as though I was on the verge of collapse. Once I got to the office, I was okay, as long as I could just sit there with my patients. My mind was working well, but my body was totally unglued.

This went on for several months. I experienced a depth of physical impairment that can only be described as a living death. As time went on, I deteriorated steadily. Slowly but surely, I was rendered physically incapable of performing each and every thing that I did in my life. The last thing to go was my work. This was what I loved doing more than anything else, and I fought hard to keep at it. But by December, I was too ill to continue working.

I left early on a Wednesday afternoon, and knew I could not go back. The fear was that I did not know if I would ever get well. What if I was never able to return to work? I was totally terrified. I had worked very hard for many years to achieve success in my practice. My profession provided me with tremendous meaning and purpose. I did not want to lose it. I decided to take one month off, focus on my health, and then re-evaluate. I called all of my patients and told them that I would have to be out of the office until January, and that I would call them towards the end of the December to reschedule their appointments. This gave me a target date to return, but also the freedom to extend my leave, if necessary.

Taking off for a month was very beneficial for me. It allowed me time to really focus on my well-being and to get to the root of the problem. I went to see several doctors about the problems I was experiencing. The first doctor basically ignored the problems I was having and told me that I was fine. I asked him if my symptoms might be related to going off the Pill, and he said he did not think so. I continued to get worse and worse. I eventually sought out another opinion.

I was then recommended to another physician at the National Naval Medical Center in Bethesda, Maryland with high hopes for resolution of the problem. I described to her in detail what I was experiencing, including the dizziness, blood sugar problems, panic attacks and debilitating depression. I asked her if this could be related to going off the Pill after taking it for twenty-five years straight. She responded with a resounding "No." She then told me that I needed to see a psychiatrist. I tried to explain to her that I myself am a psychologist and have a great understanding of these matters. I said that I knew this was not a problem of psychological origin. She dismissed what I said, and persisted in devaluing my thoughts and ideas about the problems I was having.

This experience left me feeling crushed, helpless, and hopeless. Was I ever going to be able to get help with this? Was I ever going to get better? Would I ever be my former self again? I was beginning to wonder. I felt so far off course that I knew something serious was going on. It was time to call in the big guns. I got Ron involved in helping me. Since he was a department head at the National Naval Medical Center, he was able to make rapid arrangements to assess my situation more thoroughly.

I was tested for everything imaginable. All the major, life-threatening illnesses were ruled out. This left me with the question: What was going on here? I was talking to my mother one Sunday, and she remembered that when her own mother went through menopause, she had experienced symptoms similar to mine—crying spells, anxiety, depression, and dizziness. It was my mother who finally put it together that I was going through an intensified menopause-like experience as the result of going off the Pill, which is comprised of hormones. If natural menopause caused a very minor version of what I was experiencing, then it made sense that I could be experiencing my current symptoms as the result of an acute withdrawal from the hormones. I saw an endocrinologist and it was determined that my estrogen was indeed at a low level.

I decided to take the matter to one more doctor. I saw another physician whom my husband knew personally. When I explained to her what had been happening to me over the past several months, she thought it would be worth a try to go back on the hormones and resume taking the Pill in order to alleviate my symptoms. I was in eager to do this, because I was reaching a low point of desperation. I could not take being so ill much longer. I needed a solution.

I resumed taking the Pill, and started to feel slightly better almost immediately. The difficulty was going to be, however, that hormonal problems require a very long time to resolve. This healing process would take eighteen months to two years to be fully corrected, but it would keep getting better every month. This is exactly what happened. In the months that followed, I had to learn to reintegrate myself into my own life.

This was not an easy task, because the illness had affected me in very profound ways. I had developed phobias about doing certain things, because of the vast negative memories of the preceding six months which continued to haunt me. I had painful memories of doing most of my normal everyday activities, and I was very frightened of recurrences.

At one point, I had gone grocery shopping and gotten so dizzy in the store that I could not stand up. I had to grab onto the sides of the aisles and get out of the store immediately. I then became afraid of going to grocery stores. The same thing happened at the drugstore, and at work. Every activity had to be re-experienced again repeatedly without negative consequences until I was able to function again comfortably. My stress tolerance and energy level had diminished considerably, so I really had to take tiny steps, one piece at a time.

I forced myself to face what I dreaded until the fears were gone. I challenged myself to do what was uncomfortable and scary. It got better and better. I learned that if I was afraid to do something, I could bring someone with me for support and to help me practice. Then I would eventually be able to do it alone.

As I went through this process, I felt as though I was being resurrected from death. It was a very powerful experience that gave me enormous appreciation for all the small things that I do each and every day. The abilities to stand, hear, touch, taste, and go out in the world cannot be overrated. I realized just how much I had taken for granted before my illness. I gained an appreciation for life that only comes from profound pain and loss. In many ways, the illness was a tremendous gift.

I had gained thirty pounds as a result of the hormonal imbalance. This was a bizarre experience, as I had never had any significant weight gain throughout my entire life. I had never eaten thoughtfully in the past, and had always remained petite. Now I felt like a boat. I had no clue as to how to deal with the weight gain. It was my mother's expert guidance that led me to returning to my normal weight. I wrote down my food intake daily, including portion size. I did not put one thing in my mouth without writing it down. At the end of each day, my mother and I spoke and calculated the caloric and nutritional value of the food. She taught me how to achieve balance in my diet, which ultimately translated to more balance in my life.

I came to acceptance of the fact that it was not meant for me to have a child. There was no way that I would ever consider going off the Pill again, because l was unwilling to re-experience the living hell I had just gone through as a result of going off the hormones. This was a no-brainer. I was simply not meant to get pregnant and give birth. I had felt this throughout most of my life, but there was no doubt about it now. I felt very peaceful about the resolution that was given to me by the universe. It was clear and undisputable. A very complex question had been answered by the difficulties of the past several months.

I have come to understand that there are many ways to parent in the world. It is not necessary to give birth in order to contribute to the world and make a difference in peoples' lives. We can all have many children, as well as many parents throughout our lives. For myself, I am able to parent many people through my professional life as a psychotherapist.

My patients can turn to me for help, guidance, and support in the same way that a child turns to a parent. Many people could not turn to their parents for what they needed, but are able to get what they missed in the therapeutic environment. I know that my work with patients has an effect not only upon them, but also a ripple effect upon other people in their lives. What is most important is to find a way to give to somebody, something, or a cause outside of oneself, and to feel passionate about doing so.

At times I still feel that I am an outsider because I am not part of the club of motherhood. Although I have three wonderful children through my marriage, I will not know what it feels like to give birth and raise a child from infancy. Am I still a complete woman? Can I reach my full potential without having done this? Yes. In fact, my potential may even be increased in some ways as the result of not having had a baby.

There are many advantages to not having had children. I retain enormous freedom in my life that I would not otherwise have. I also have more comfort, financial security, and the capacity to have great adventures. There is space and time available for creative endeavors, such as writing. I can focus on living my own life fully and contributing to the world in a broader capacity than I would be able to if I had the responsibilities of raising children. I am also able to focus more on nurturing the well-being of my marriage.

At midlife, one grieves the paths not taken, regardless of which paths actually have been taken. This is an unavoidable passage in healthy psychological development. Regardless of the choices we have made, we re-evaluate them when we become aware that our time is limited, and that certain options are no longer available. I will always wonder what my biological son or daughter would have been like. If I had it to do all over again, I would probably choose to make the same decisions, because I needed to make all of those choices in order to become the person who I am today.

17

TRADING ROLE-
PLAYING FOR REALITY

When I was in my thirties, I was focused on school, building a new career, and making a success of myself in the world. I was taken in by outside things. It was important to look good and have all the right trappings. I was sober but because my recovery work had lessened, I began making people, places, and things my God. I had lost my connection with myself and my own spiritual connection. My quest to achieve and prove my worth became greater then my need to be myself.

At this time, I was dating Patrick, who had a fondness for porn. When he revealed this to me, I was not self-confident enough to take it for what it was. I felt insecure and threatened. I thought that I was not adequate, and not good enough. I wanted to be as desirable as the girls on film. I wanted to have to what they had that men wanted. It was as though I felt that I had to compete with people I did not even know for something I did not even know I wanted.

I was given naturally gorgeous breasts. They were small, but firm, and proportionate for my 5'2" 100-pound size. When I was young, I did not even need to wear a bra. I felt whole and complete, and best of all, sexy. I had never had any sexual difficulties, and had always felt desired by the opposite sex. I had had many boyfriends and lovers from all walks of life throughout my years, and felt that sexuality was a natural and healthy gift of being alive.

I started asking women friends if they had ever considered getting implants. I discovered that many of my friends had already done so, and I did not even know it. I had two girlfriends who had recently gotten breast implants, and were very happy with the results. They bragged to me about their boob jobs, and I felt envious.

I asked myself if getting breast implants would make me feel better about myself, and I thought that the answer was "yes." I decided rather impulsively that I should do it too, in order to measure up. I wanted to be consistent with the standards that I perceived were being held by society to be beautiful. I made an appointment with one of Washington's top doctors, and within a week, scheduled surgery for myself.

The surgery went very well. I was left with a pair of saline-filled breasts, which had gone from an "A" cup to a "C" cup. I felt very proud and feminine with my big pair of new breasts. This was something I had never imagined that I would ever do. On a whim, it was done. I was informed by my doctor that I would probably need follow-up surgery at some point in the future to replace the implants. There were risks, but I was not concerned. Those bad outcomes happened rarely, I told myself. I would be fine. I would cross the bridge of additional surgery if and when I ever came to it.

For the first week, I was in intense physical agony. I had never dreamt that it was going to be so painful. The soreness was gut-wrenching. I needed painkillers for valid reasons. This is a challenge for someone in recovery, because there are relapse and addiction risks involved with taking addictive medications, even when they are really required. I took less pain medicine than I actually needed, and paid a big price for it. I was so scared of triggering a relapse that I suffered more then I had to. As it turned out, I was responsible about taking the medication. I took it as directed, and for less time than I actually needed it. I had been sober for many years at that point and was not close to going back to using, even though it was my old favorite class of drugs, opiates.

It took a few months for the swelling to subside. I was not sure what to expect. The outcome was that my new breasts were gorgeous and natural-looking. This happened right around the time that I broke it off with Patrick and got together with Ron. Ron was the first person to see them. He gushed over them, and I felt that I had done a good thing. Although it had been triggered by my then-boyfriend Patrick, my new husband would reap the benefits and deserved to do so. After all, he had married me.

As time went by, I never quite got comfortable with my breasts, although they were physically beautiful and a surgical success. There had been no problems or side effects. However I no longer felt like me. I felt top heavy, which made me feel weighty in general. When I looked at photos of myself, I looked older and more matronly than I had before the surgery. I no longer felt pretty, young, and light. The reality was that I actually was getting older, but the surgery had adversely impacted my feeling of comfort in my own skin. I felt as though I was someone else, and I did not like it.

After a few years, I talked to Ron about my feelings. He confessed to me that he did not really like breast implants, but mine were the best he had ever seen. Ron did not like fake things. He said that he had kept his mouth shut about it because I had already had the surgery before we got together. He felt that there was no point in his being negative about it. He had gushed over my breasts when he first saw them because he gushed over everything about me. He always loved and adored every little thing about me, and always will. I was mistaken to think that he had found me sexy because of my new fake breasts. It was me he loved, not the breasts.

As time went on, I felt less and less comfortable as the transporter of the saline implants. I finally made a decision to have them removed. I had heard about people who had experienced bad surgical outcomes who had them removed, but never anyone who had such beautiful implants. Mine were perfect; I just did not want them. I wanted to feel like me again.

Ron helped me find the best surgeon for the job, and I had them removed. The surgery went quite smoothly. As I left the hospital, I remember feeling unburdened and feeling like myself again for the first time in years. I felt pretty again. My posture straightened up, and my physical and psychological equilibrium were re-established. My clothes fit better, and I felt lean and mean again. I was back.

I could not be authentic with the implants because I had constructed a false self. Something had to change. I had gotten the implants for the "other" and not for me. The "other" is someone outside of yourself whom you are trying to please or compete with. When we construct our identity in the gaze or view of the "other," we are constructing a false self. This self is one that we think we need to be in order to gain approval from those around us. The false self is one that is constructed in order to be seen, rather than to just be.

Instead of being who we really are, we can get caught up in being what we think we are supposed to be. Many of our choices are fueled by having to look a certain way, in order to play a particular role in life. All of this is perpetuated by the media, advertising, and our highest cultural icons: actors. The people that we look up to the most in this culture are those who literally play a part as a means of earning a living, movie stars. When is it time to exchange role-playing for reality?

It all began for me when I was twelve years old, and my father told me I had skinny legs. I wanted his approval to such a great extent that for almost two decades I never again wore a dress or a skirt, with the exception of my required school uniform. I had adopted his criticism of my legs as gospel, to which I required myself to pay respect. I spent years at the gym exercising and working out my legs and calf muscles. When I finally started to wear skirts at the age of thirty, I constantly got compliments on my legs. How could this be? Had my dad been wrong? Had my legs gotten better? It became clear to me that I had been living my life based on the view of the "other," rather than authentically.

One of the most authentic women I have ever met is a gorgeous Prussian businesswoman in Washington named Inge. Inge, a diplomat's wife, has lived all over the world—Germany, Paris, and London, in addition to Washington. She is physically beautiful, as well as elegant, dynamic and magnetic. She has been one of my greatest teachers of dignity, elegance, and classic style. Inge is a fashion Ubermensch. She owns a clothing store that is one of Washington's best-kept secrets. She exquisitely guides her clients to become the best version of themselves. Having vast expertise with people, Inge understands and reads individuals well. She brings much needed European flair and knowhow to the American market.

Inge knows who she is and does not want to be anybody else. She would never consider dying her hair or having plastic surgery. Why? She loves herself too much to change herself. She knows that she is beautiful exactly the way she is, and is ultra confident. Like many European women, she understands that being natural is what makes a woman beautiful. She would never risk damaging her exquisite authentic self with surgical alteration. Inge is a role model for all women who want to be fabulous, elegant, and real.

My first encounter with Inge was in her store. I walked up the steps, and was greeted by her exclamation, "You are the most beautiful woman who has ever been in this store." She did not care that there were other women in the store who heard her comment to me and may have felt diminished. It was love at first sight. We adored each other. I felt a chemistry and synergy with her that has endured over many years. Not only did she help me to become a well-heeled professional, but her enchanting spirit also became part of my consciousness. This was perhaps the greatest gift of all. We have had many wonderful conversations over the years, including one which led to my writing this book:

Inge said to me, "Dr. Anita, you must write a book."
"Why?" I asked.

"You have a lot to say and a wonderful way of expressing yourself. You will help a lot of people. You must give birth to a book."

Throughout our conversations, Inge always told me exactly what I needed to hear at precisely the time I needed to hear it. Many times, when I felt insecure about myself or my choices, Inge complimented and affirmed the very thing that I was worried about. It has been uncanny. Thus, I did not take her words about writing the book lightly.

I had been thinking about writing for many years. I had loved to write as a child, and had lost my practice of doing so when I started using drugs and alcohol. It was only natural that writing, like so many other lost parts of my selfhood, would return at some point in sobriety. I did not know when I would do it, but I always knew that I would write again. Her prompting gave me the nudge that I needed to begin.

Inge's guidance has also helped me develop my own sense of style. When I was younger, I spent inordinate amounts of money buying the latest trends to try to keep up with what I thought was needed in order to be fashionable. It is easy to become a victim of the media and marketing entrepreneurs every season, always feeling that you need something else in order to be complete. I have learned that it is not about buying what is in style at the moment and trying to be like everyone else. It is more important to find out who you really are, what works for you, and sticking with that.

In my case, I prefer classic styles in a few basic colors that can be easily mixed and matched. I am petite, so I need to keep it simple. My wardrobe needs to be professional, functional and versatile, yet high quality and classic. This means that inexpensive items can be mixed with higher-end basics, along with interesting accessories. Quality, not quantity is the guiding principle. I would rather purchase one excellent piece of clothing per season than five inexpensive trendy ones. Over the years, I have built up a classic collection of clothes that reflect my inner self. I do not need to change with the trends every year in order to try to fit in. Beauty and glamour are about finding who you really are, and making the most of that.

I see so many women in our society who are imprisoned by feeling obligated to measure up to an external physical ideal. We are told we must look a certain way, dress to play a particular part, and have such and such in order to be complete. This leaves us with a chronic feeling of emptiness, which can only then be temporarily alleviated by further purchases and physical improvements. When are we okay? When are we ever going to be enough? Is this another form of addiction?

What I now realize is that I was never deficient. Removing the implants was a milestone in my journey to becoming authentic. Through this act, I made the statement to myself that I am enough. I do not have to be something other than who I am. Since then, I have continued on that journey. It has evolved from one that began with external changes to one that is now more internal and spiritual. As time has gone on, the changes have come at deeper and deeper levels. I have continued to make choices that are guided by my own soul, rather than by what I perceive to be the expectations of others. I have been inwardly directed towards more profound levels of honesty, integrity, and self-directedness. I continue to make more choices that are driven by a sense of purpose and meaning.

18

LIFE AND DEATH

In December of 2005, Ron and I went to Paris for the Christmas holidays. We spent several days in the fashionable district of St. Germain de Pres; eating, shopping, watching people, and savoring the culture. We had the most romantic and magnificent trip that either one of us had ever taken in our lives. We were booked to go from Paris to London for the New Year and reluctantly left Paris for our next destination. It was painful to leave Paris. We both wanted more.

So the next Christmas, we decided to go back to Paris, and stay for a longer time. This time we would be in Paris for over a week. As December of 2006 was approaching, we were both excited about our upcoming trip. We had been looking forward to it for an entire year. However, early December was filled with quite a few stresses at home in dealing with our regular life. By the time we left for Paris, I was completely depleted.

I had a vague intuition that this trip was not going to be smooth. I did not know why. I was frightened of something going wrong on the trip, and had been catastrophizing in my mind prior to leaving. I imagined countless scenarios in which we would be in grave difficulty. For some reason, I did not feel safe. I was inclined to chalk it up to stress and keep moving forward. I hoped that the trip would be rejuvenating, restful, and restorative.

When we arrived in Paris at the Hotel St. Germain des Pres, we nestled into our room. I had opted for the smallest room available. The previous year, we had rented a full suite, and were out of the room the entire day, every day. This time, it seemed like a waste to get anything bigger than a basic room to sleep in. Our room was fully equipped but extremely compact, as much of Paris tends to be. The king-sized bed took up most of the space in the quarters. You could barely walk around the bed to the small, newly renovated bathroom. The color theme was crimson, with an old-style French feeling.

The first couple of days were fun and reminiscent of the previous year. We walked around St. Germain, St. Michel, the Champs Elysees, and enjoyed the city. We tried to go to the Louvre, but the lines were so long that we gave up. Everywhere we went, there were massive international crowds of visitors for the Christmas holidays. We found English-speaking recovery meetings, and went to one every day. This was exciting, as we got to hear a new and diverse crowd of people speaking in the meetings. Many people there were passing through on vacation, as we were.

On the third day we met up with our friend Dick, from Washington. He was a former American diplomat, and had settled permanently in Paris. We went to dinner at a famous restaurant that specializes in seafood. I ate their legendary platter of raw oysters, with six different types of oysters from around the globe. What a special treat. This appetizer was followed by fresh sautéed fois gras, and dessert. We had a lovely evening. After dinner, we strolled through the streets of Paris. Dick knew the city very well, and graciously showed us around.

When we got back to the hotel, I did not feel very well. I got extremely weak and dizzy, and was very sick to my stomach. Something unexpected had hit me. All of the life force drained out of me. This was big. I was very confused and surprised about what was happening. What was this? I felt as though I was literally going to leave my body. It was like my spirit and energy were being sucked out of my body by a vacuum. I actually remember the moment when I thought to myself, "This is it. I'm leaving the planet for good." I knew that this was what it must feel like to die. It was a chilling and surreal moment that will forever be suspended in time in my memory.

I started to collapse, and then vomited for the entire night. It dawned on me that I had gotten a case of food poisoning. This was not the first time I had ever had this experience in my life. I had suffered through the same type of occurrence about twenty years prior from eating bad mussels in Baltimore. At that time, I had gotten violently ill; however, it had passed after a day or two. I had been sick and vomiting, but once the toxins were released, I felt fairly normal and was able to resume my regular life.

I thought that this would probably be similar. I anticipated losing a day or two from the vacation, and then getting back to the business of having fun. Enjoying this trip was not optional; it was my only big vacation that year. Between the lack of revenue from taking off and the actual expenses of the trip, it had also cost a fortune. I absolutely could not have a bad time that week.

The next day, I could not move. I was so ill that I was bedridden. Not only my stomach, but my entire system was fighting my body. There was an internal nuclear war going on and no one was winning. I could not get any food down or keep anything at all in my system. I felt horribly out of sync with my body. I was frightened and did not know when this was going to let up.

I got chills and fever over the next few days, and continued to have no energy whatsoever. This persisted longer than I had expected. I still could not eat much or move about. Ron brought me crepes from the corner street vendor, which I attempted to choke down. I tried to go out to eat and shop, but had to quickly return to the miniature crimson hotel room where I had anticipated spending no time at all, except to sleep.

I was in terrible shape. I could not leave the room at all. The chills and fever did not go away. Fortunately, I was traveling with Ron, who was formerly an emergency and critical care doctor. He always traveled with a full supply of emergency meds in the event that anything like this ever happened. We guessed that I probably did not need to go to the hospital, and Ron treated me accordingly. I started on a powerful course of antibiotics. Again, I hoped that things would clear up soon and that we could salvage at least a few days of the vacation.

There was not a lot to do in the room. Lying there day after day was very depressing. There was a television with very restricted reception. Thus, my choices were limited. Saddam Hussein had just been executed, and the footage of his death was the main event on French television that week. Every channel was carrying the story, and replayed the execution over and over again. I tried to read in order to distract myself, but my eyes could not focus. Thus, there was little else to do other than to watch television. The repetitive impact of the Saddam Hussein story was not helping my spirits. After seeing him put to death hundreds of times, I felt like dying myself.

A new issue crept up. I had developed a pain in my inner ear. Ron thought that perhaps because of the intense vomiting, some toxic fluid had traveled into the wrong tube in my ear, causing an ear infection. The issue that this presented was that it might not be safe to fly. If I had an ear infection and flew, there was a risk of bursting my ear drum. This would not be good. A therapist who cannot hear will not be able to work very effectively. I was even more terrified. I feared that my entire life as I knew it was being taken away.

This trip had turned into a nightmare; I did not know when it would be safe to travel back to Washington. I just wanted to go home and get into my own bed. I longed for home sweet home. I felt safe in Washington, and knew how the medical system worked. I did not know how to deal with this serious an illness in a foreign country. It seemed like an insurmountable task to try to figure it all out, especially in my current condition. Where should I go and whom could I trust? I was terrified that I would never make it home. I just wanted to get the hell out of France. I wanted to get out and never go back again.

This was in sharp contrast to the way I had felt my entire life. Paris had always been my paradise. I grew up studying the French language for seventeen years, and had idolized the French culture and way of life. I sought out relationships with French people in order to be closer to the culture. I had been totally in love with Paris over my lifetime, but now Paris and I were having our first lovers' quarrel. I hated Paris. It felt like a God-awful place that was trying to kill me. I never wanted to come there again. Because of all the terrifying memories, I became quite conflicted about ever going back.

Even after eight days, I was still severely ill. I was able to eat very little, and was extremely weak and disoriented. Eventually, Ron and I made the decision that we would fly home. We were not sure if this was the right thing to do at the time, but we followed our intuition. Sometimes, intuition is all you've got. Ron gave me an additional steroid medication to help me get home safely. I could not pack fast enough. I remember the feeling of relief as we were in the taxi on the way to the airport. If only I could get home, I thought that I would get better. Being in Paris was a curse.

I flew home with enormous trepidation about my eardrums bursting. The prospect of losing my hearing meant facing possible loss of employment, income, and the ability to meet the responsibilities that kept my life going. Ron tried to establish that flying at this time was reasonably safe, and showed me how to clear the passageways from my ears by holding my nose and blowing until air cleared the opening. I said a prayer as we took off. Everything seemed to be okay. I was still able to hear. Fortunately, the flight home was uneventful. No problems. I could still hear. Thank God.

After arriving in Washington, I again expected that I would soon return back to my previous state of good health prior to the trip. Ron and I were exhausted, depleted, and disappointed, but delighted to be home. After all, this was the place I thought I would never see again. I thought that once the jetlag was over, things would fall back into place. This turned out not to be the case.

As the subsequent weeks passed, I was not doing well. My energy level was poor, and I was still having major problems with my left ear, which was aching and itching. I heard a constant ringing sound. It was a struggle to get through each day. I had patients scheduled from morning until evening, and felt depleted by the afternoon. As a therapist, it is very important to sustain good health and positive energy in order to work most effectively. I wanted to be myself again.

I experienced dizzy spells while driving, which terrified me. The dizziness was reminiscent of my previous major illness a few years earlier from the hormone deficiency. This triggered many of the feelings I had experienced several years prior; anxiety, hopelessness, and fear. I was not going through hormone deficiency again, but I was dizzy and had emotional flashbacks. I needed to know that this was something different, and that it would pass.

After another month, I went to an ENT specialist, who examined me and said that I did indeed have a blockage in one ear that could be causing the dizziness. He treated the condition promptly. Once I knew what the problem was, I felt relieved. However, the fatigue and weakness persisted. I did not expect this to continue for so long. Ron did some research and discovered that while in Paris, I had contracted "Vibrio Vulnificus," a fatal form of food poisoning. More than fifty percent of people who contract this toxin die.

It was all coming together. Initially, I did not know what had happened, and made reasonable, but incorrect assumptions that prevented me from seeking adequate medical help immediately. Had I known the full story, I would have immediately gone to the hospital in France. I was extremely fortunate to have survived this episode. If I did not have luck on my side and been in good physical health, I may not have made it. I always thought that it would be very poetic to die in Paris, but not at such a young age. I never actually expected it to almost happen. Be careful what you wish for.

The healing process from the food poisoning took three months, which was much longer than I had anticipated. During this time, I progressively got better. Slowly, my energy level returned and I began to feel like myself again. Coming out of this ordeal set into motion a new consciousness and love of life that I had never had before. It put me into a state of living fully and savoring each day. Although I had made strides forward after coming out of my health difficulties three years prior, this time it was even more profound.

I started to really live as I never had before, and took more responsibility for my own happiness. I had previously been living my life on a treadmill. It was all about work. I would go through the work week, and then do little else on the weekends to have fun. I was too lazy, complacent, and tired to make an effort for myself. I was spending a lot of time talking with others about living life, but what about mine? I had forgotten about it.

I had become somewhat isolated as the result of letting my life get out of balance. I was enjoying my work, but not much else in my life. I realized that life could end at any given time, through no fault of my own. Never before did I really understand this at my core. What did I want my life to be? What was really important to me? How did I want to spend my time? I realized that you can get money back, but you can never get time back.

I came to an acceptance about death and dying. It is not a question of "if;" it is a question of "when?" Since I do not know the answer to that question, I need to live my life to the fullest every single day. What is it that makes life full? It is not about money, power, and prestige. It is about people and giving what you can. A rich life is a peopled life. I remembered that the best times in my life had been the times when my life was well-peopled. How did I lose this? How had I become so isolated without even knowing it?

I believe that the answer to this question lies at the heart of addiction issues. Addiction is a disease of isolation, loneliness, and being out of touch with the truth. Even though I had not taken a drink or drug for seventeen years, I was still affected by the underlying disease of addiction. You do not have to be actively using for the disease to still have a negative impact on you. I was sober, but isolated, lonely, and dishonest with myself. I needed to make major changes in my life.

One of the first major changes I made was to stop watching television. Instead of watching other people live life, I decided to start living my own. This freed up quite a bit of time in my schedule. This time was then channeled into many other constructive and fulfilling activities. I had no idea how much time was being eaten up by television until I stopped watching it. Television puts you in a passive position and is isolating. Rather than being active, you are passively sitting or lying back, and not participating in life.

It is very easy to become cut off from life without even realizing it. Watching television is not a substitute for interacting with other real live human beings. In my opinion, it can contribute significantly to depression. As we become more active, we feel more empowered by life. I found that there was a direct correlation between the amount of television that I watched and my mental health. Technology can be used either to connect more with others, or to isolate. It is crucial to make thoughtful choices.

Reading, which is still a relaxing activity, is much healthier because it requires effort and mental action. I realized that due to the aging process, I would probably not have good eyesight forever. This increased my desire to read and learn as much as possible, while I still can. The time that I used to spend in front of the television is now spent reading, writing, talking with people, improving my professional knowledge, exploring and enjoying life, and enriching my mind.

After the near-death experience, I began to write this book. For many years, I had felt in the back corners of my mind that I would write, but I did not know exactly when. After a pivotal conversation with Inge in which she encouraged me to start writing, I was guided from within to begin. I started by reading books about how to write a book. This was crucial, because I needed guidance. Those books helped me to understand the basics and to formulate the concept for my book. It is always easier to learn the ropes from people who have already been there. Why reinvent the wheel?

I then decided to begin the writing process before my forty-fifth birthday. My goal was to write one page per day, which required roughly one hour daily. This was doable. I certainly could find one hour each day for a project that was so important to me. Sometimes, I wrote first thing in the morning, other days it was during the day when I had an unexpected break or in the evening. I have always been able to make time for things that really matter to me. This was one of them.

I found that the writing process feeds on itself. Once you begin, you get into a flow of creativity that taps into an energy source that comes from a place deep within. The writing process is slow, natural and cannot be forced or rushed. It must unfold in the way it is supposed to. On some days, the stream of ideas is strong and furious, while on other days, it dribbles out. Just like life itself, it is not a perfect process.

Accessing my creative energy has been enormously joyful and empowering. I have always used creative energy in my work as a therapist, but focusing on a large creative project was different. It gave me something that was my own powerfully unique creation. It profoundly changed my feeling about living. When I started writing, I got the sense that this was something that I had needed, but had been missing for a long time in my life. Writing has made me more balanced, grateful, happy, generous, and independent.

I remember seeing my grandfather, who was a renowned author, writing all the time when he came to visit us from India. He would wake up at three o'clock in the morning and sit at my mother's dining table to write whenever the spirit moved him. I could see his passion, and even shared it with him when I was young. I had been a writer as a child but had lost my interest in writing when I started drinking. After seventeen years of sobriety, my desire to write returned. It was another thing that my addiction had stolen from me. But I got it back.

As a result of my near-death experience in Paris, I was brought to life. Instead of merely existing, I really started to live. My spirit was awakened into a new dimension. Although this had happened several times before in my life, this time it happened at an even deeper level. What does not kill us makes us stronger. In my case, death awareness has made me come alive.

19

BECOMING A THERAPIST

I remember wanting to be a therapist when I was six years old. Perhaps this stemmed from the early childhood feelings of chaos and confusion that resulted from my parents' divorce. I wanted to make sense of it all. I wanted to get them back together, and help them to work it out. If only I could say the right words, things might be okay.

There are always reasons why we make our choices. I believe that out of our greatest difficulties can also come our greatest gifts. Throughout the fifteen years of my addiction, I lost touch with myself. I was unable to connect with my own sprit and essence. After being sober for a little while, I started to find my true self again. I became the person that I was meant to be all along, and would have been sooner if I had not gotten so trapped in my addiction.

When I started graduate school in sobriety, I knew I was on the right path. I could feel it in my soul, and there was no doubt whatsoever. I knew that I wanted to be a psychotherapist and work in private practice. I am grateful for the clarity that I eventually received, even though it took so long to come. On my second day in class, my professor told us that it was extremely difficult to make it in private practice, and that managed care had ruined it for therapists. We might as well forget it, she said. As an impressionable student, I was mortified. Should I not be in this graduate program? Was this all a mistake? Had I made a grievous error in planning? She could not possibly be correct. At least, I hoped she was not.

I decided to move forward in faith. I actually knew therapists who were making it quite well in private practice. How could she be right? I asked my own therapist how much money she made, and learned that she did quite well financially. I met a couple of other students who were like me. They wanted to be therapists in order to help people, but they also wanted to be successful in their own practices.

I came to understand that there are many viewpoints, and that I need to stay close to people who either want what I want, or have what I want. If I wanted to be able to have a practice of my own, I needed people in my life who were of the same mind. I ultimately worked harder and pushed further beyond my limits because I wanted to prove my professor wrong. She actually turned out to be a great gift in my journey.

Throughout graduate school, I made straight A's. I devoted myself to my newfound purpose as I had never committed myself to anything, except using. The same energy that fueled my addiction was now being channeled in a constructive way. I began to see what I could really do if I tried to live up to my potential. As I neared the end of school, I was confronted with choices about what to do next.

I had gotten married to someone in my field that had a lot more experience than I did. This was infinitely helpful for me. I was able to discuss my options and choices with a seasoned mentor, as well as his colleagues. One night I was at a recovery meeting, and had heard about Kolmac Clinic, a substance abuse treatment center in the area. The next day, I asked Ron about it, and he just happened to have the medical director's card in his pocket. What an amazing coincidence, I thought.

I called there and spoke to Mary, one of the clinical directors, to explore whether or not they had any openings for clinicians. It just so happened that my timing was perfect. There was a staff member who was about to leave, and they needed a counselor. On the phone, I was asked about the origin of my interest in substance abuse treatment and recovery issues. I hesitated. I did not know whether or not I should reveal that I was in recovery. Would this hurt my credibility as a professional? I was afraid that if I revealed the truth, it would be held against me. I was reluctant. I paused, and then spoke the truth.

Mary sounded pleased. She said that she was glad that I was in recovery. She made it clear that the clinic preferred to hire people who were in recovery themselves, because they were more effective in working with patients. The only issue was whether the prospective hire had a stable and lengthy enough sobriety. I did. Whew. I was relieved. I had been honest, done the right thing, and it had worked in my favor. I got the job.

At the same time, I started my own private practice in Georgetown. I decided to start my practice in an unusual way. One evening, Ron and I had gone to a gypsy fortune-teller in Georgetown. She read my palm, and made vague predictions about my future. She asked me what I did, and I told her that I was a psychotherapist. She told me that she needed help herself, and asked if I would be willing to take her on as a patient. I agreed, and my practice was born in that moment. She was my first patient. After that, my clientele built up slowly, but steadily.

Because of my marital difficulties, I had gotten back into therapy myself. I had developed a good relationship with Paul, my therapist, who was about to retire and move out of state. During one of our sessions he mentioned his future plans to me. As an offhand remark, I asked him to let me know when he was going to leave, because I would be delighted to take over his practice. At the time I did not think he would ever take me up on that. After all, I was his patient, and he was my therapist. We had a defined and established therapeutic relationship. When the time came for Paul to retire, I got an unexpected phone call:

"Are you still interested in taking over my practice?"

"Absolutely, I am." I was thrilled. "When are you going to be leaving?" I now had mixed emotions, because I realized that I was also losing my therapist.

"I'll be leaving in about three or four months."

"How should we go about doing this?"

"I'll draw up a contract, you can go over it, and then we'll see what we need to figure out."

"That sounds great. Have you told your patients?"

"Not yet; I'm planning to start telling them closer to when I leave 1. I will get back to you with a contract proposal in the next week or so."

I could not believe that this was really happening. How had I had such good timing? I felt so lucky to have this opportunity. Not only was I going to take over his practice, but also his office space at a prime location in Bethesda, along with all the office equipment and furniture. Sometimes, when something remarkable happens, the universe in winking at you.

I now had to make the transition from being Paul's patient to being his business associate. This was a huge change in our relationship. I was losing my therapist, but gaining something I needed even more, a business mentor. He was an excellent clinician as well as business person, and taught me the intricacies of running a practice effectively. I learned about marketing, scheduling, billing, and professional development. Part of our contract was for ongoing supervision of cases that had been transitioned, so I had a continuing professional relationship with Paul after he left. It was not a bad time to take a break from therapy. Things at home were stabilizing, and I was now focused primarily on building my career.

By the time the practice had changed hands, I was running full steam ahead. I now had two offices. I had my original office in Washington, and now a second location in Maryland. I was also still working at the clinic as well. The clinic was my home base; so I had the security of some outside employment to carry me through the transition to self-employment. Although I was stretched as far as possible, it was clear that the direction I was taking was the right one. My dream was to work on my own, for myself, in my own practice. I knew that I was meant to be self-employed. Throughout my journey, I had questioned whether it could really happen for me. Now my vision was being realized one piece at a time.

I eventually cut down on my hours at the clinic, and steadily increased my hours in my own practice. In the beginning, I took any work that came my way, for any fee. My goal was to fill my schedule as much as possible. For a brief time, I joined insurance panels, but quickly came to the realization that that was not for me. Working with the insurance companies was unnerving and frustrating to no end. I wanted a practice that would allow me to focus on patient care, rather than on the business of trying to get paid for my services. The only way to achieve this was to take control of the things I could. This meant cutting out the middleman. I decided that it was better to have fewer self-pay patients than a high volume of insurance referrals. I was willing to be patient, and to build my practice the most effective way for me.

This was the first business decision that I had made that really reflected self-care. You can only take care of your practice as well as you take care of yourself. I was willing to build my practice more slowly, but more in accordance with my values. I chose not to settle for less than I wanted. This is essential not only in business, but in life.

How many choices had I made in my life based on what I thought I was supposed to do, rather than what I really wanted in my life? How many jobs had I chosen because I though they sounded good on paper, but were not the least bit fulfilling or interesting to me? How many men had I been involved with because they looked good, but did not make me feel good? If I was going to have my own business, I needed it to reflect what I really wanted.

As time went on, my practice grew steadily. I got referrals from a variety of professionals and colleagues. I learned something new every day. Patients teach you as much as you teach them. At the end of every day, I felt excited and alive. I knew I was doing what I was really meant to do. Building my practice was an ongoing process of both clinical and business education, as well as learning about the interplay between the two. I realized how little my training had prepared me for private practice and working with patients. Although I had the best education money could buy, as well as several top-notch internships, there was nothing like being in the real world.

It also became clear how everything I had ever done up to this point had prepared me for my professional life as a therapist. Working in restaurants and bars had given me people skills. Working in my father's law firm had given me expertise in managing an office. Working in hotels and in sales had given me discipline and drive. My many years of education had given me clinical training and experience. The clinical supervision from other professionals had expanded and refined my knowledge. My own addiction had given me extraordinary expertise with alcoholism and addictions that no learning institution could ever teach.

In the past, I had questioned why I was stuck in some of the dead-end, no-win situations that I had been in. Now it all came together. For the first time, my life began to made sense. I could see how I needed all of my past experiences to reach the point of really being able to help others and make a difference in their lives.

When I first entered the mental health field, I was not inclined to work with patients with addiction and recovery issues. I felt that I had spent enough time and energy focusing on that subject. I thought I wanted to specialize in another area, but I did not know which one. I sought a new focus of interest in my life. During my training, however, I did not abide by this thought. I naturally gravitated to research projects involving different aspects of addiction. This persisted throughout my entire training. Once I had gone down that road, I continued to be led from within in the same direction. I was given opportunity after opportunity to deepen my clinical knowledge and training in the substance abuse field. Whatever I had originally thought I wanted did not matter. The universe was going to make use of me as it saw fit.

What I knew about addiction and alcoholism could only be learned by having been there, and then having recovered from it. Very few other professionals in the field could offer this. In fact, many of my patients reported that other professionals whom they saw did not really understand addiction and alcoholism. A vast number of my patients had not been served very well in the past by the medical profession because of the general lack of understanding about addiction issues. I began to realize that I had something valuable to contribute.

As a therapist, every session is an adventure. You never knew what is going to happen. You never know what will come out of the mouths of your patients. Sometimes patients adore you, and others hate you. At times, you have personal reactions to them, and cannot allow your personal feelings to affect your clinical judgment. There are some patients who make enormous progress, while others stay stuck. The progress depends not only on the skill of the therapist, but also on the patient's motivation and willingness to keep working for change.

I believe that it is important not to over-identify with the role of the all-knowing expert. Patients do seek help from therapists and want guidance, but our answers may not be their answers. People must experience everything that they choose in order to arrive at the point of readiness for change. As a therapist, I can help them to move along through this process. My role is to help the patient to perceive reality, identify choices, go through his own process, and ultimately find his own answers.

As a therapist, you simultaneously examine the patient's needs and progress, yourself, and everything else that occurs in the clinical sessions. This is the essential work of being a therapist. Examination of the patient is secondary only to examination of oneself. How can you possibly help someone else if you are not helping yourself and working on your own issues as well? Being a therapist is a profession that has continued to foster my own personal and professional growth. Every year, I can assess enormous progress from the previous year.

I continue, even after seventeen years of continuous sobriety, to attend recovery meetings on a daily basis. I continue to work with my own therapist and advisors. I have also expanded my own personal work into different areas of growth, including relationship, money, and food issues. Relationship issues had always been insurmountable for me prior to recovery. After getting married, I knew that I needed to get additional help with codependency, or I would end up divorced. Although I never had serious problems with money or food, I am well aware that once substance abuse is arrested, addiction can easily migrate into other areas of life. It is important to stay on top of all aspects of my life, and to try to keep them in balance.

I have found that the better care I take of myself, the better care I am able to take of my practice and my patients. Thus, it has been essential to build self-care time into my daily schedule and routine. In private practice, it is very tempting to take on more and more and more, because you are never really sure if there will be more business coming your way around the corner. This can lead to poor-quality work and burnout, which is deadly for a therapist.

My daily morning routine begins with ten minutes of meditation, followed by five minutes of yoga, and then twenty minutes of exercise. I then get ready, go to a morning recovery meeting, and to the office. I have learned that it is essential to take breaks during the day. I reserve a chunk of time at midday to eat, write, attend part of another meeting, do errands, or socialize with friends. After working for a few hours in the afternoon, I take another break, and then see a few more patients in the evening. By the end of the day, I have achieved a balance between giving to others and giving to myself. Through structure and discipline comes freedom.

One of the most challenging aspects of being in private practice is the isolation that comes from working alone. It is crucial to be affiliated with other professionals. I have maintained a relationship with my professional family-of-origin at the Kolmac Clinic. Once a week, I do a therapy group there, and have the opportunity to interact with other professionals. In addition to running the group at the clinic, I have also started my own peer supervision group for medical professionals who are also in recovery. These activities have created balance in my life and reduced the isolation that can occur when a clinician is working independently.

It is an honor and a joy to be an intimate part of peoples' lives. I cannot imagine a better occupation. If the source of all suffering is thinking of self, and the source of all joy is thinking of others, then psychotherapy is the perfect profession. A therapist has the opportunity to get out of himself, and think about others all day long. And sometimes, even make a difference.

In some ways, psychotherapy is also the impossible profession. There is no perfection. There is no end to the work that needs to be done in order for human beings to live their lives to the fullest. As soon as one challenge is mastered, life changes, and another challenge takes its place. You can never please everybody. You are the constant recipient of patients' unresolved psychological issues and conflicts with people from their past. You never know what to expect, so you cannot plan for it. This is where the art comes in. Not only do we work with a scientific body of knowledge, but we are also artists, crafting every session to the patients' best interest.

I have had many professional opportunities that I never imagined possible. In 1999, I had the opportunity to serve as a consultant to the United States Congress for parity in substance abuse legislation. In February, 2000, I was a primary presenter at the Tokyo Conference on Addictions. I spoke to four hundred physicians and therapists in

Tokyo, Japan about the therapeutic use of self-help programs by psychotherapists in the treatment of addictive disorders. In 2003, I was a featured speaker at a national convention for family members of alcoholics and addicts. I have also spoken on radio, television, and in the press.

I have had the most wonderful patients that anyone could hope for. From unemployed alcoholics to high-functioning elected officials, I have found the work exhilarating and exciting. It has been expansive and far-reaching. On most days, I go home with a glow. I think I probably learn just as much from my patients as they do from me, if not more.

20
EXPANDING HORIZONS

Feeling like an outsider throughout life has compelled me to strive to seek meaning, find truth, and develop spiritually. Initially, feeling like an outsider made me try to avoid reality, which caused me to lose my connection with myself and everything around me. Even during the drinking days, I always knew deep inside that it was essential to feel a part of something greater than myself. Since my instincts were misguided, I went about seeking this ineffectively. I used my addictions to try to feed my spiritual hunger.

In recovery, trying to deal with my unrelenting sense of loneliness has made my life full and rich. It has continually forced me to reach out to others, instead of staying trapped within myself. Part of the underlying disease that fueled my addiction is the natural tendency to close up and isolate. Left to my own devices, this comes very naturally to me. I am responsible to fight this tendency each day. I must consciously seek connection with others in order to get out of myself. Just because I do it today does not mean that I will not have to do it again tomorrow. I will. Thus, I must practice this daily, on an ongoing basis.

Over time, I have cultivated a life that is abundant in every way. My family life has undergone miraculous healing. My relationship with my mother is perhaps the greatest miracle of all. For so many years during my addiction, she and I were either in severe conflict or estranged. In recovery, our relationship has grown closer and closer as time has passed. We have become best friends who cherish one another. There is nothing we cannot discuss together. My father and I had always had a close relationship, but it was interrupted by the divorce. After moving in with him in high school, I was able to connect with him deeply and fulfill my need for closeness with him. In recovery, our relationship has evolved to a mature, adult-adult father-daughter relationship. He is truly a great friend and confidante, and we can also discuss absolutely anything openly.

Although my parents did divorce, I was able to spend ten years living with each of them and developing close relationships with both. These relationships have become richer with time. I am beginning to see how the best of both of my parents was passed on to me. From my mother, I got discipline, strong values, intellect, a loving heart, great sensitivity and an enormous capacity for feeling. From my father, I was given a sharp and intelligent mind, courage, charisma, joie de vivre, curiosity, and openness. It is easy to identify your parents' shortcomings, but much more important to identify their gifts and contributions to your life. I am truly grateful for both of them.

As a result of recovery, there has also been healing in my relationships with extended family. I have come to appreciate and cultivate relationships with relatives that are all over the world. After visiting India in sobriety, I truly became part of my family of origin. Since then, several of my cousins have moved to this country and have settled here. In the Indian culture, cousins are considered the equivalent of brothers and sisters; so I do not feel as alone as I once did.

I have been able to integrate my two cultures within myself and my life. I no longer feel that I have to choose. Am I American or Indian? I am just me. I am an American of Indian descent, which means that internally, I am a blend of both worlds. This results in a much richer understanding of the world than I would otherwise have. It also renders me a unique package. How many Indian-American, recovering addict, Quaker-Hindu-Buddhist therapists do you know?

My marriage has been a gift of sobriety. Ron and I never would have met if we had not both been in recovery. We probably would have both remained single and searching for the rest of our lives. Most importantly, we would not still be married if we had not both been active in recovery and willing to work on our own issues. Because of recovery, it is possible to start a relationship in trauma, but later flourish in love.

Both of us have gone beyond where we ever imagined possible in a relationship. We both also believe that our relationship has made it possible for each of us to progress much further as individuals. When you are not busy trying to medicate your loneliness with people, it is possible to focus on other activities and interests. I am very grateful to be part of his wonderful and large family, and to have step-children. We both know that we are able to contribute more to the world because we are together than we could if we were apart. Maybe that is why the universe has kept us together through thick and thin.

In addition to my family of origin, I also have a recovery family. These are people whom I have known for varying lengths of time. Some of them have been in my life for almost two decades. We came out of the womb together and grew up in sobriety. Others are new friends who are on the same path. Still others are people whom I have yet to meet. This family is available to me anywhere, anytime, all over the world.

The joy of recovery friends is that we reach out to each other as a way of life. We must seek connection with one another in order to survive. Recovery friends understand you at a very intimate level, regardless of how long you have known them. They have all been where you are in one way or another. There are so many levels upon which we automatically relate because of where we have been with addiction. Another bonus is that new people keep coming into your life. How many middle-aged professionals can keep on making new and intimate friends all the time? We are very lucky.

I am also in touch with many of my old friends who are not in recovery. Over time, we have grown and changed dramatically, but still share the deep roots that only a life-time of relationship can create. I am much more present to them than I ever was before sobriety. Making other new friends has also been enriched by sobriety. It is true that people seek their own level in relationships. As I have gotten healthier, I can see how more high quality people have come into my life than ever before.

I am very grateful for the work that I do. Every day, I feel lucky to be there. It is exciting, interesting, and keeps me growing and learning. I am a much more effective therapist because of all of the experiences that I have had. It is easy to read about issues and difficulties, but it is much more powerful to have been there and found your way out of the darkness. I am able to connect with my patients on a deep and human level. I respect them enormously, and feel that everyone is capable of living up to their potential if they work on it. People really can change and grow. That is what living is all about. If you do not believe that, you might as well hang it up now.

It is easy to regret the past and focus on opportunities that were missed as a result of addiction. I find it more productive to focus on the here and now. It is what I can do today that is important. Everything that happened in the past needed to happen in order to bring me to the point where I am now. I needed every drink I had. I needed every experience and learning opportunity, especially the disasters. It is sometimes through crisis that one is given the greatest gifts of all.

I always loved to live on the edge. Before my recovery, so many of my experiences were rooted in staying on the edge. The edge of life, sanity, health, the world, and myself. Sobriety has brought me into equilibrium. The abundance of life comes from having balance and fulfillment in many different spheres. I have been given the chance to develop in many different areas, and am still doing so. Finding balance has been a very imperfect process. In my case, it has usually involved going from one extreme to the other, before ending up in the middle. It is not through the extremes that life is fulfilling. It is not about more and more and more. More of anything is not really going to make me happy. It is focusing on what I have now that will bring authentic joy. Keeping it all in balance is what will make my life abundant.

Although it has not been an easy journey, it has been wonderful. The spiritual journey is often undertaken as the result of pain and difficulties. At every turn, we have the choice to try to face our issues, or to run away. Facing the challenges often requires the willingness to experience excruciating emotions for as long as it takes to move through them in order to get to the other side. It is getting to the other side that ultimately brings us to the healing. We must go through the pain to get to the healing and to grow spiritually.

I used to think that my feelings would kill me. This was an incorrect assumption that was based in profound fear and a lack of experience in dealing with life as it really is. Getting into recovery started me on my journey, but that was only the beginning. It was not enough to just not drink or take a drug. I first had to learn how to live again, and then develop myself in other ways in order to find my true self. I had to figure out who I really was, and how I could make a difference in the world. Sometimes you have to try on different selves in order to find out who you are not.

Finding meaning has been crucial to my life. Discovering a way to give back is essential. It is not just about achieving external success and getting what you want; it is also about giving. That is not to say that money is not important. Money matters. But it is not enough to fulfill a person. As my wise uncle Ram says, "If you want to be happy, make other people happy." Getting out of self is the central task of living a spiritually-centered life.

For me, finding a way to nurture others through work that I love has provided me the opportunity to feel a sense of meaning day after day. There are many ways to find meaning, and it is important that we each find our own path. That road does not have to be the same for everyone, and it does not have to fit a societal mold. It just has to fit who we are. Discovering who we are is the journey.

Just as alcoholism and addiction had a destructive impact on every part of my life, recovery has had positive effects on all aspects of my existence. Recovery continues to take me beyond where I have ever been before in every area of my life. With ongoing work, I can continue to develop my potential infinitely. I am living at a higher level than even one year ago; emotionally, physically, and spiritually.

This enables me to focus more clearly on how I can make a difference in the lives of others. I continue to see more and more possibilities for making meaning of my life. Living up to my potential was initially defined by merely learning how to live. Now it means reaching out beyond my own world, and finding new ways to contribute and make a difference. It continues to grow and change. Contributing to the world at a higher level is a gift of recovery that has taken many years to recognize and cultivate. The horizon keeps expanding.

978-0-595-46689-4
0-595-46689-3

Lightning Source UK Ltd.
Milton Keynes UK
27 January 2010

149199UK00001B/132/A